The Richest Man in Babylon

The Richest Man in Babylon

George S. Clason

WAKING LION PRESS

ISBN 978-1-4341-0445-8

Published by Waking Lion Press, an imprint of The Editorium
Waking Lion Press™, the Waking Lion Press logo, and The Editorium™
are trademarks of The Editorium, LLC

The Editorium, LLC
West Jordan, UT 84081-6132
wakinglionpress.com
wakinglion@editorium.com

Contents

vi

Preface

Ahead of you stretches your future like a road leading into the distance. Along that road are ambitions you wish to accomplish . . . desires you wish to gratify.

To bring your ambitions and desires to fulfillment, you must be successful with money. Use the financial principles made clear in the pages which follow. Let them guide you away from the stringencies of a lean purse to that fuller, happier life a full purse makes possible.

Like the law of gravity, they are universal and unchanging. May they prove for you, as they have proven to so many others, a sure key to a fat purse, larger bank balances, and gratifying financial progress.

LO, MONEY IS PLENTIFUL FOR THOSE WHO UNDERSTAND THE SIMPLE RULES OF ITS ACQUISITION:

Start your purse to fattening.
Control your expenditures.
Make your gold multiply.
Guard your treasures from loss.
Make of your dwelling a profitable investment.
Insure a future income.
Increase your ability to earn.

Introduction

Our prosperity as a nation depends upon the personal financial prosperity of each of us as individuals.

This book deals with the personal successes of each of us. Success means accomplishments as the result of our own efforts and abilities. Proper preparation is the key to our success. Our acts can be no wiser than our thoughts. Our thinking can be no wiser than our understanding.

This book of cures for lean purses has been termed a guide to financial understanding. That, indeed, is its purpose: to offer those who are ambitious for financial success an insight which will aid them to acquire money, to keep money, and to make their surpluses earn more money.

In the pages which follow, we are taken back to Babylon, the cradle in which was nurtured the basic principles of finance now recognized and used the world over.

To new readers the author is happy to extend the wish that its pages may contain for them the same inspiration for growing bank accounts, greater financial successes, and the solution of difficult personal financial problems so enthusiastically reported by readers from coast to coast.

To the business executives who have distributed these tales in such generous quantities to friends, relatives, employees, and associates, the author takes this opportunity to express his gratitude. No endorsement could be higher than that of those who appreciate its teachings because they, themselves, have worked up to important successes by applying the very principles it advocates.

Babylon became the wealthiest city of the ancient world because its citizens were the richest people of their time. They appreciated the value of money. They practiced sound financial principles in acquiring money, keeping money, and making their money earn more money. They provided for themselves what we all desire . . . incomes for the future.

G. S. C.

A Historical Sketch
of Babylon

In the pages of history there lives no city more glamorous than Babylon. Its very name conjures visions of wealth and splendor. Its treasures of gold and jewels were fabulous. One naturally pictures such a wealthy city as located in a suitable setting of tropical luxury, surrounded by rich natural resources of forests and mines. Such was not the case. It was located beside the Euphrates River, in a flat, arid valley. It had no forests, no mines—not even stone for building. It was not even located upon a natural trade-route. The rainfall was insufficient to raise crops.

Babylon is an outstanding example of the human ability to achieve great objectives, using whatever means are at our disposal. All of the resources supporting this large city were man-developed. All of its riches were man-made.

Babylon possessed just two natural resources—a fertile soil and water in the river. With one of the greatest engineering accomplishments of this or any other day, Babylonian engineers diverted the waters from the river by means of dams and immense irrigation canals. Far out across that arid valley went these canals to pour the life-giving waters over the fertile soil. This ranks among the first engineering feats known to history. Such abundant crops as were the reward of this irrigation system the world had never seen before.

Fortunately, during its long existence, Babylon was ruled by successive lines of kings to whom conquest and plunder were but incidental. While it engaged in many wars, most of these were local or defensive against ambitious conquerors from other countries who coveted the fabulous treasures of Babylon. The outstanding rulers of Babylon live in history because of their wisdom, enterprise, and justice. Babylon produced no strutting monarchs who sought to conquer the known world that all nations might pay homage to their egotism.

As a city, Babylon exists no more. When those energizing human forces that built and maintained the city for thousands of years were withdrawn, it soon became a deserted ruin. The site of the city is in Asia about six hundred miles east of the Suez Canal, just north of the Persian Gulf. The latitude is about thirty degrees above the Equator, practically the same as that of Yuma, Arizona. It possessed a climate similar to that of this American city, hot and dry.

Today, this valley of the Euphrates, once a populous irrigated farming district, is again a windswept, arid waste. Scant grass and desert shrubs strive for existence against the windblown sands. Gone are the fertile fields, the mammoth cities, and the long caravans of rich merchandise. Nomadic bands of Arabs, securing a scant living by tending small herds, are the only inhabitants. Such it has been since about the beginning of the Christian era.

Dotting this valley are earthen hills. For centuries, they were considered by travelers to be nothing else. The attentions of archaeologists were finally attracted to them because of broken pieces of pottery and brick washed down by the occasional rainstorms. Expeditions, financed by European and American museums, were sent to excavate and see what could be found. Picks and shovels soon proved these hills to be ancient cities. City graves, they might well be called.

Babylon was one of these. Over it, for something like twenty centuries, the winds had scattered the desert dust. Built originally of brick, all exposed walls had disintegrated and gone back to earth once more. Such is Babylon, the wealthy city, today. A heap of dirt, so long abandoned that no living person even knew its name until it was discovered by carefully removing the refuse of centuries from the streets and the fallen wreckage of its noble temples and palaces.

Many scientists consider the civilization of Babylon and other cities in this valley to be the oldest of which there is a definite record. Positive dates have been proved reaching back 8000 years. An interesting fact in this connection is the means used to determine these dates. Uncovered in the ruins of Babylon were descriptions of an eclipse of the sun. Modern astronomers readily computed the time when such an eclipse, visible in Babylon, occurred and thus established a known relationship between their calendar and our own.

In this way, we have proved that 8,000 years ago, the Sumerites, who inhabited Babylonia, were living in walled cities. One can only conjecture for how many centuries previous such cities had existed. Their inhabitants were not mere barbarians living within protecting walls. They were an educated and enlightened people. So far as written history goes, they were the first engineers, the first astronomers, the first mathematicians, the first financiers and the first people to have a written language.

Mention has already been made of the irrigation systems which transformed the arid valley into an agricultural paradise. The remains of these canals can still be traced, although they are mostly filled with accumulated sand. Some of them were of such size that, when empty of water, a dozen horses could be ridden abreast along their bottoms. In size they compare favorably with the largest canals in Colorado and Utah.

In addition to irrigating the valley lands, Babylonian engineers completed another project of similar magnitude. By means of an elaborate drainage system they reclaimed an immense area of swamp land at the mouths of the Euphrates and Tigris Rivers and put this also under cultivation.

Herodotus, the Greek traveler and historian, visited Babylon while it was in its prime and has given us the only known description by an outsider. His writings give a graphic description of the city and some of the unusual customs of its people. He mentions the remarkable fertility of the soil and the bountiful harvest of wheat and barley which they produced.

The glory of Babylon has faded but its wisdom has been preserved for us. For this we are indebted to their form of records. In that distant day, the use of paper had not been invented. Instead, they laboriously engraved their writing upon tablets of moist clay. When completed, these were baked and became hard tile. In size, they were about six by eight inches, and an inch in thickness.

These clay tablets, as they are commonly called, were used much as we use modern forms of writing. Upon them were engraved legends, poetry, history, transcriptions of royal decrees, the laws of the land, titles to property, promissory notes and even letters which were dispatched by messengers to distant cities. From these clay tablets we are permitted an insight into the intimate, personal affairs of the people. For example, one tablet, evidently from the records of a country storekeeper, relates that upon the given date a certain named customer brought in a cow and exchanged it for seven sacks of wheat, three being delivered at the time and the other four to await the customer's pleasure.

Safely buried in the wrecked cities, archaeologists have recovered entire libraries of these tablets, hundreds of thousands of them.

One of the outstanding wonders of Babylon was the immense walls surrounding the city. The ancients ranked them with the great pyramid of Egypt as belonging to the "seven wonders of the world." Queen Semiramis is credited with having erected the first walls during the early history of the city. Modern excavators have been unable to find any trace of the original walls. Nor is their exact height known. From mention made by early writers, it is estimated they were about fifty to sixty feet high, faced on the outer side with burnt brick and further protected by a deep moat of water.

The later and more famous walls were started about six hundred years before the time of Christ by King Nabopolassar. Upon such a gigantic scale did he plan the rebuilding, he did not live to see the work finished. This was left to his son, Nebuchadnezzar, whose name is familiar in Biblical history.

The height and length of these later walls staggers belief. They are reported upon reliable authority to have been about one hundred and sixty feet high, the equivalent of the height of a modern fifteen story office building. The total length is estimated as between nine and eleven miles. So wide was the top that a six-horse chariot could be driven around them. Of this tremendous structure, little now remains except portions of the foundations and the moat. In addition to the ravages of the elements, the Arabs completed the destruction by quarrying the brick for building purposes elsewhere.

Against the walls of Babylon marched, in turn, the victorious armies of almost every conqueror of that age of wars of conquest. A host of kings laid siege to Babylon, but always in vain. Invading armies of that day were not to be considered lightly. Historians speak of such units as 10,000 horsemen, 25,000 chariots, 1200 regiments of foot soldiers with 1000 men to the regiment. Often two or three years of preparation would be required to assemble war materials and depots of food along the proposed line of march.

The city of Babylon was organized much like a modern city. There were streets and shops. Peddlers offered their wares through residential districts. Priests officiated in magnificent temples. Within the city was an inner enclosure for the royal palaces. The walls about this were said to have been higher than those about the city.

The Babylonians were skilled in the arts. These included sculpture, painting, weaving, gold working and the manufacture of metal weapons and agricultural implements. Their Jewelers created most artistic jewelry. Many samples have been recovered from the graves of its wealthy citizens and are now on exhibition in the leading museums of the world.

At a very early period when the rest of the world was still hacking at trees with stone-headed axes, or hunting and fighting with flint-pointed spears and arrows, the Babylonians were using axes, spears and arrows with metal heads.

The Babylonians were clever financiers and traders. So far as we know, they were the original inventors of money as a means of exchange, of promissory notes and written titles to property.

Babylon was never entered by hostile armies until about 540 years before the birth of Christ. Even then the walls were not captured. The story of the fall of Babylon is most unusual. Cyrus, one of the great conquerors of that period, intended to attack the city and hoped to take its impregnable walls. Advisors of Nabonidus, the king of Babylon, persuaded him to go forth to meet Cyrus and give him battle without waiting for the city to be besieged. In the succeeding defeat to the Babylonian army, it fled away from the city. Cyrus, thereupon, entered the open gates and took possession without resistance.

Thereafter the power and prestige of the city gradually waned until, in the course of a few hundred years, it was eventually abandoned, deserted, left for the winds and storms to level once again to that desert earth from which its grandeur had originally been built. Babylon had fallen, never to rise again, but to it civilization owes much.

The eons of time have crumbled to dust the proud walls of its temples, but the wisdom of Babylon endures:

Money is the medium by which earthly success is measured.

Money makes possible the enjoyment of the best the earth affords.

Money is plentiful for those who understand the simple laws which govern its acquisition.

Money is governed today by the same laws which controlled it when prosperous citizens thronged the streets of Babylon, six thousand years ago.

The Man Who Desired Gold

Bansir, the chariot builder of Babylon, was thoroughly discouraged. From his seat upon the low wall surrounding his property, he gazed sadly at his simple home and the open workshop in which stood a partially completed chariot.

His wife frequently appeared at the open door. Her furtive glances in his direction reminded him that the meal bag was almost empty and he should be at work finishing the chariot, hammering and hewing, polishing and painting, stretching taut the leather over the wheel rims, preparing it for delivery so he could collect from his wealthy customer.

Nevertheless, his fat, muscular body sat stolidly upon the wall. His slow mind was struggling patiently with a problem for which he could find no answer. The hot tropical sun, so typical of this valley of the Euphrates, beat down upon him mercilessly. Beads of perspiration formed upon his brow and trickled down unnoticed to lose themselves in the hairy jungle on his chest.

Beyond his home towered the high terraced wall surrounding the king's palace. Nearby, cleaving the blue heavens, was the painted tower of the Temple of Bel. In the shadow of such grandeur was his simple home and many others far less neat and well cared for. Babylon was like this—a mixture of grandeur and squalor, of dazzling wealth and direst poverty, crowded together without plan or system within the protecting walls of the city.

Behind him, had he cared to turn and look, the noisy chariots of the rich jostled and crowded aside the sandaled tradesmen as well as the barefooted beggars. Even the rich were forced to turn into the gutters to clear the way for the long lines of slave water carriers, on the "King's Business," each bearing a heavy goatskin of water to be poured upon the hanging gardens.

Bansir was too engrossed in his own problem to hear or heed the confused hubbub of the busy city. It was the unexpected twanging of the strings from a familiar lyre that aroused him from his reverie. He turned and looked into the sensitive, smiling face of his best friend—Kobbi, the musician.

"May the gods bless you with great liberality, my good friend," began Kobbi with an elaborate salute. "Yet, it appears they have already been so generous that you need not labor. I rejoice with you in your good fortune. More, I would even share it with you. Pray, from your purse which must be bulging, else you would be busy in your shop, extract but two humble shekels and lend them to me until after the feast this night. You will not miss them before they are returned."

"If I did have two shekels," Bansir responded gloomily, "to no one could I lend them—not even to you, my best of friends; for they would be my fortune—my entire fortune. No one lends his entire fortune, not even to his best friend."

"What!" exclaimed Kobbi with genuine surprise. "You have not one shekel in your purse, yet you sit like a statue upon a wall! Why not complete that chariot? How else can you provide for your noble appetite? 'Tis not like you, my friend. Where is your endless energy? Does something distress you? Have the gods brought to you troubles?"

"A torment from the gods it must be," Bansir agreed. "It began with a dream, a senseless dream, in which I thought I was a man of means. From my belt hung a handsome purse, heavy with coins. There were shekels which I cast with careless freedom to the beggars; there were pieces of silver with which I did buy finery for my wife and whatever I did desire for myself; there were pieces of gold which made me feel assured of the future and unafraid to spend the silver. A glorious feeling of contentment was within me! You would not have known me for your hardworking friend. Nor would have known my wife, so free from wrinkles was her face and shining with happiness. She was again the smiling maiden of our early married days."

"A pleasant dream indeed," commented Kobbi, "but why should such pleasant feelings as it aroused turn you into a glum statue upon the wall?"

"Why, indeed! Because when I awoke and remembered how empty was my purse, a feeling of rebellion swept over me. Let us talk it over together, for, as the sailors say, we ride in the same boat, we two. As youngsters, we went together to the priests to learn wisdom. As young men, we shared each other's pleasures. As grown men, we have always been close friends. We have been contented subjects of our kind. We have been satisfied to work long hours and spend our earnings freely. We have earned much coin in the years that have passed, yet to know the joys that come from wealth, we must dream about them. Bah! Are we more than dumb sheep? We live in the richest city in all the world. The travelers say none equals it in wealth. About us is much display of wealth, but of it we ourselves have naught. After half a lifetime of hard labor, you, my best of friends, have an empty purse and say to me, "May I borrow such a trifle as two shekels until after the noblemen's feast this night?" Then, what do I reply? Do I say, "'Here is my purse; its contents will I gladly share?' No, I admit that my purse is as empty as yours.

What is the matter? Why cannot we acquire silver and gold—more than enough for food and robes?

"Consider also our children," Bansir continued. "Are they not following in the footsteps of their parents? Need they and their families and their children's families live all their lives in the midst of such treasurers of gold, and yet, like us, be content to banquet upon sour goat's milk and porridge?"

"Never, in all the years of our friendship, did you talk like this before, Bansir." Kobbi was puzzled.

"Never in all those years did I think like this before. From early dawn until darkness stopped me, I have labored to build the finest chariots anyone could make, soft-heartedly hoping that someday the gods would recognize my worthy deeds and bestow upon me great prosperity. This they have never done. At last, I realize this they will never do. Therefore, my heart is sad. I wish to be a person of means. I wish to own lands and cattle, to have fine robes and coins in my purse. I am willing to work for these things with all the strength in my back, with all the skill in my hands, with all the cunning in my mind, but I wish my labors to be fairly rewarded. What is the matter with us? Again I ask you! Why cannot we have our just share of the good things so plentiful for those who have the gold with which to buy them?"

"Would I knew an answer!" Kobbi replied. "No better than you am I satisfied. My earnings from my lyre are quickly gone. Often I must plan and scheme that my family be not hungry. Also, within my breast is a deep longing for a lyre large enough that it may truly sing the strains of music that surge through my mind. With such an instrument I could make music finer than even the king has heard before."

"Such a lyre you should have. No one in all Babylon could make it sing more sweetly; not only the king but the gods themselves would be delighted. But how may you secure it while both of us are as poor as the king's slaves? Listen to the bell! Here they come." He pointed to the long column of half-naked, sweating water-bearers plodding laboriously up the narrow street from the river. Five abreast they marched, each bent under a heavy goatskin of water.

"A fine figure of a man, he who leads them." Kobbi indicated the wearer of the bell who marched in front without a load. "A prominent man in his own country, 'tis easy to see."

"There are many good figures in the line," Bansir agreed. "Tall, blond men from the north, laughing black men from the south, little brown men from the nearer countries. All marching together from the river to the gardens, back and forth, day after day, year after year. Naught of happiness to look forward to. Beds of straw upon which to sleep—hard grain porridge to eat. Pity the poor brutes, Kobbi!"

"Pity them I do. Yet, you make me see how little better off are we, free though we call ourselves."

"That is true, Kobbi, unpleasant thought though it be. We do not wish to go on year after year living slavish lives. Working, working, working! Getting nowhere."

"Might we not find out how others acquire gold and do as they do?" Kobbi inquired.

"Perhaps there is some secret we might learn if we but sought from those who knew," replied Bansir thoughtfully.

"This very day," suggested Kobbi, "I passed our old friend, Arkad, riding in his golden chariot. This I will say, he did not look over my humble head as many in his station might consider his right. Instead, he waved his hand that all onlookers might see him pay greetings and bestow his smile of friendship upon Kobbi, the musician."

"He is claimed to be the richest man in all Babylon," Bansir mused.

"So rich that the king is said to seek his golden aid in affairs of the treasury," Kobbi replied.

"So rich," Bansir interrupted, "I fear if I should meet him in the darkness of the night, I should lay my hands upon his fat wallet"

"Nonsense," reproved Kobbi, "a man's wealth is not in the purse he carries. A fat purse quickly empties if there be no golden stream to refill it. Arkad has an income that constantly keeps his purse full, no matter how liberally he spends."

"Income, that is the thing," ejaculated Bansir. "I wish for an income that would keep flowing into my purse whether I sit upon the wall or travel to far lands. Arkad must know how to make such an income. Do you suppose it is something he could make clear to a mind as slow as mine?"

"I think he taught his knowledge to his son, Nomasir," Kobbi responded. "Did he not go to Nineveh and, so it is told at the inn, become, without aid from his father, one of the richest citizens of that city?"

"Kobbi, you bring to me a rare thought." A new light gleamed in Bansir's eyes. "It costs nothing to ask wise advice from a good friend, and Arkad was always that. Never mind though our purses be as empty as the falcon's nest of a year ago. Let that not detain us. We are weary of being without gold in the midst of plenty. We wish to become men of means. Come, let us go to Arkad and ask how we also may acquire incomes for ourselves."

"You speak with true inspiration, Bansir. You bring to my mind a new understanding. You make me realize the reason why we have never found any measure of wealth. We never sought it! You have labored patiently to build the staunchest chariots in Babylon. To that purpose was devoted your best endeavors. Therefore, at it you did succeed. I strove to become a skillful lyre player. And, at it I did succeed.

"In those things toward which we exerted our best endeavors we succeeded. The gods were content to let us continue thus. Now, at last, we see a light, bright like that from the rising sun. It bids us to learn more that we may prosper more. With a new understanding we shall find honorable ways to accomplish our desires."

"Let us go to Arkad this very day," Bansir urged. "Also, let us ask other friends of our boyhood days, who have fared no better than ourselves, to join us, that they too may share in this wisdom."

"You were ever thus thoughtful of your friends, Bansir. Therefore you have many friends. It shall be as you say. We go this day and take them with us."

The Richest Man in Babylon

In old Babylon there once lived a certain very rich man named Arkad. Far and wide he was famed for his great wealth. Also was he famed for his liberality. He was generous in his charities. He was generous with his family. He was liberal in his own expenses. Nevertheless, each year his wealth increased more rapidly than he spent it.

And there were certain friends of younger days who came to him and said: "You, Arkad, are more fortunate than we. You have become the richest man in all Babylon while we struggle for existence. You can wear the finest garments and enjoy the rarest foods, while we must be content if we can clothe our families in raiment that is presentable and feed them as best we can.

"Yet once we were equal. We studied under the same master. We played in the same games. And in neither the studies nor the games did you outshine us. And in the years since, you have been no more an honorable citizen than we.

"Nor have you worked harder or more faithfully, insofar as we can judge. Why, then, should a fickle fate single you out to enjoy all the good things of life and ignore us who are equally deserving?"

Thereupon Arkad remonstrated with them, saying, "If you have not acquired more than a bare existence in the years since we were youths, it is because you either have failed to learn the laws that govern the building of wealth, or else you do not observe them.

"'Fickle Fate' is a vicious goddess who brings no permanent good to anyone. On the contrary, she brings ruin to almost everyone upon whom she showers unearned gold. She makes wanton spenders, who soon dissipate all they receive and are left beset by overwhelming appetites and desires they have not the ability to gratify. Yet others whom she favors become misers and hoard their wealth, fearing to spend what they have, knowing they do not possess the ability to replace it. They are further beset by fear of robbers and doom themselves to lives of emptiness and secret misery.

"Others there probably are, who can take unearned gold and add to it and continue to be happy and contented citizens. But so few are they, I know of them but by hearsay. Think you of those who have inherited sudden wealth, and see if these things are not so.

"His friends admitted that of the people they knew who had inherited wealth these words were true, and they besought him to explain to them how he had become possessed of so much prosperity, so he continued: "In my youth I looked about me and saw all the good things there were to bring happiness and contentment. And I realized that wealth increased the potency of all these.

"Wealth is a power. With wealth many things are possible.

"One may ornament the home with the richest of furnishings.

"One may sail the distant seas.

"One may feast on the delicacies of far lands.

"One may buy the ornaments of the gold worker and the stone polisher.

"One may even build mighty temples for the gods.

"One may do all these things and many others in which there is delight for the senses and gratification for the soul.

"And, when I realized all this, I decided that I would claim my share of the good things of life. I would not be one of those who stand afar off, enviously watching others enjoy. I would not be content to clothe myself in the cheapest raiment that looked respectable. I would not be satisfied with poverty. On the contrary, I would make myself a guest at this banquet of good things.

"Being, as you know, the son of a humble merchant, one of a large family with no hope of an inheritance, and not being endowed, as you have so frankly said, with superior powers or wisdom, I decided that if I was to achieve what I desired, time and study would be required.

"As for time, all men have it in abundance. You, each of you, have let slip by sufficient time to have made yourselves wealthy. Yet, you admit: you have nothing to show except your good families, of which you can be justly proud.

"As for study, did not our wise teacher teach us that learning was of two kinds: the one kind being the things we learned and knew, and the other being the training that taught us how to find out what we did not know?

"Therefore I decided to find out how one might accumulate wealth, and when I had found out, to make this my task and do it well. For is it not wise that we should enjoy while we dwell in the brightness of the sunshine, for sorrows enough shall descend upon us when we depart for the darkness of the world of spirit?

"I found employment as a scribe in the hall of records, and long hours each day I labored upon the clay tablets. Week after week, and month after month, I labored, yet for my earnings I had nothing to show. Food and clothing and penance to the gods, and other things of which I could not remember, absorbed all my earnings. But my determination did not leave me.

"And one day Algamish, the money lender, came to the house of the city master and ordered a copy of the Ninth Law, and he said to me, I must have this in two days, and if the task is done by that time, two coppers will I give to you."

"So I labored hard, but the law was long, and when Algamish returned, the task was unfinished. He was angry, and had I been his slave, he would have beaten me. But knowing the city master would not permit him to injure me, I was unafraid, so I said to him, 'Algamish, you are a very rich man. Tell me how I may also become rich, and all night I will carve upon the clay, and when the sun rises it shall be completed.'

"He smiled at me and replied, 'You are a forward knave, but we will call it a bargain.'

"All that night I carved, though my back pained and the smell of the wick made my head ache until my eyes could hardly see. But when he returned at sunup, the tablets were complete.

"'Now,' I said, 'tell me what you promised.'

"'You have fulfilled your part of our bargain, my son,' he said to me kindly, 'and I am ready to fulfill mine. I will tell you these things you wish to know because I am becoming an old man, and an old tongue loves to wag. And when the young come to the aged for advice, they receive the wisdom of years. But too often does youth think that age knows only the wisdom of days that are gone, and therefore profits not. But remember this: the sun that shines today is the sun that shone when your father was born, and will still be shining when your last grandchild shall pass into the darkness.

"'The thoughts of youth,' he continued, 'are bright lights that shine forth like the meteors that oft make brilliant the sky, but the wisdom of age is like the fixed stars that shine so unchanged that sailors may depend upon them to steer their course.

"'Mark you well my words, for if you do not, you will fail to grasp the truth that I will tell you, and you will think that your night's work has been in vain.'

"Then he looked at me shrewdly from under his shaggy brows and said in a low, forceful tone, 'I found the road to wealth when I decided that a part of all I earned was mine to keep. And so will you.'

"Then he continued to look at me with a glance that I could feel pierce me but said no more.

"'Is that all?' I asked.

"'That was sufficient to change the heart of a sheep herder into the heart of a money lender,' he replied.

"'But all I earn is mine to keep, is it not?' I demanded.

"'Far from it,' he replied. 'Do you not pay the garment-maker? Do you not pay the sandal-maker? Do you not pay for the things you eat? Can you live in Babylon without spending? What have you to show for your earnings of the past month? What for the past year? Fool! You pay everyone but yourself. Dullard! You labor for others. As well be a slave and work for what your master gives you to eat and wear. If you kept for yourself one-tenth of all you earn, how much would you have in ten years?'

"My knowledge of the numbers did not forsake me, and I answered, 'As much as I earn in one year.'

"'You speak but half the truth,' he retorted. 'Every gold piece you save is a slave to work for you. Every copper it earns is its child that can also earn for you. If you would become wealthy, then what you save must earn, and its children must earn, that all may help give you the abundance you crave.

"'You think I cheat you for your long night's work,' he continued, 'but I am paying you a thousand times over if you have the intelligence to grasp the truth I offer you.

"'A part of all you earn is yours to keep. It should not be less than a tenth no matter how little you earn. It can be as much more as you can afford. Pay yourself first. Do not buy from the clothes-maker and the sandal-maker more than you can pay out of the rest and still have enough for food and charity and penance to the gods.

"'Wealth, like a tree, grows from a tiny seed. The first copper you save is the seed from which your tree of wealth shall grow. The sooner you plant that seed, the sooner shall the tree grow. And the more faithfully you nourish and water that tree with consistent savings, the sooner may you bask in contentment beneath its shade.'

"So saying, he took his tablets and went away.

"I thought much about what he had said to me, and it seemed reasonable. So I decided that I would try it. Each time I was paid I took one from each ten pieces of copper and hid it away. And strange as it may seem, I was no shorter of funds than before. I noticed little difference as I managed to get along without it. But often I was tempted, as my hoard began to grow, to spend it for some of the good things the merchants displayed, brought by camels and ships from the land of the Phoenicians. But I wisely refrained.

"A twelfth month after Algamish had gone, he returned and said to me, 'Son, have you paid yourself not less than one-tenth of all you have earned for the past year?'

"I answered proudly, 'Yes, master, I have.'

"'That is good,' he answered beaming upon me, 'and what have you done with it?'

"'I have given it to Azmur, the brickmaker, who told me he was traveling over the far seas, and in Tyre he would buy for me the rare jewels of the Phoenicians. When he returns we shall sell these at high prices and divide the earnings.'

"'Every fool must learn,' he growled, 'but why trust the knowledge of a brickmaker about jewels? Would you go to the breadmaker to inquire about the stars? No, by my tunic, you would go to the astrologer, if you had power to think. Your savings are gone, youth; you have jerked your wealth-tree up by the roots. But plant another.

Try again. And next time if you would have advice about jewels, go to the jewel merchant. If you would know the truth about sheep, go to the shepherd. Advice is one thing that is freely given away, but watch that you take only what is worth having. Those who take advice about savings from one who is inexperienced in such matters shall pay with their savings for proving the falsity of their opinions.' Saying this, he went away.

"And it was as he said. For the Phoenicians are scoundrels and sold to Azmur worthless bits of glass that looked like gems. But, as Algamish had bid me, I again saved each tenth copper, for now I had formed the habit and it was no longer difficult.

"Again, twelve months later, Algamish came to the room of the scribes and addressed me. 'What progress have you made since last I saw you?'

"'I have paid myself faithfully,' I replied, 'and my savings I have entrusted to Agger the shieldmaker, to buy bronze, and each fourth month he pays me the rental.'

"'That is good. And what do you do with the rental?'

"'I have a great feast with honey and fine wine and spiced cake. Also I have bought me a scarlet tunic. And some day I shall buy me a young ass upon which to ride.'

"To which Algamish laughed. 'You do eat the children of your savings. Then how do you expect them to work for you? And how can they have children that will also work for you? First get you an army of golden slaves, and then many a rich banquet may you enjoy without regret.' So saying he again went away.

"Nor did I see him again for two years, when he once more re-turned and his face was full of deep lines and his eyes drooped, for he was becoming a very old man. And he said to me, 'Arkad, have you yet achieved the wealth you dreamed of?'

"And I answered, 'Not yet all that I desire, but I have some, and it earns more, and its earnings earn more.'

"'And do you still take the advice of brickmakers?'

"'About brickmaking they give good advice,' I retorted.

"'Arkad,' he continued, 'you have learned your lessons well. You first learned to live upon less than you could earn. Next you learned to seek advice from those who were competent through their own experiences to give it. And, lastly, you have learned to make gold work for you.

"'You have taught yourself how to acquire money, how to keep it, and how to use it. Therefore, you are competent for a responsible position. I am becoming an old man. My sons think only of spending and give no thought to earning. My interests are great and, I fear, too much for me to look after. If you will go to Nippur and look after my lands there, I shall make you my partner and you shall share in my estate.'

"So I went to Nippur and took charge of his holdings, which were large. And because I was full of ambition and because I had mastered the three laws of successfully handling wealth, I was able to greatly increase the value of his properties. So I prospered much, and when the spirit of Algamish departed for the sphere of darkness, I shared in his estate as he had arranged under the law." So spake Arkad, and when he had finished his tale, one of his friends said, "You were indeed fortunate that Algamish made of you an heir."

"Fortunate only in that I had the desire to prosper before I first met him. For four years did I not prove my definiteness of purpose by keeping one-tenth of all I earned? Would you call a fisherman lucky who for years so studied the habits of the fish that with each changing wind he could cast his nets about them? Opportunity is a haughty goddess who wastes no time with those who are unprepared."

"You had strong willpower to keep on after you lost your first year's savings. You are unusual in that way," spoke up another.

"Willpower!" retorted Arkad. "What nonsense. Do you think willpower gives one the strength to lift a burden the camel cannot carry, or to draw a load the oxen cannot budge? Willpower is but the unflinching purpose to carry a task you set for yourself to fulfillment. If I set for myself a task, be it ever so trifling, I shall see it through. How else shall I have confidence in myself to do important things? Should I say to myself, 'For a hundred days as I walk across the bridge into the city, I will pick up a pebble and cast it into the stream,' I would do it. If on the seventh day I passed by without remembering, I would not say to myself, Tomorrow I will cast two pebbles which will do as well.' Instead, I would retrace my steps and cast the pebble. Nor on the twentieth day would I say to myself, 'Arkad, this is useless. What does it avail you to cast a pebble every day? Throw in a handful and be done with it.' No, I would not say that nor do it. When I set a task for myself, I complete it. Therefore, I am careful not to start difficult and impractical tasks, because I love leisure."

And then another friend spoke up and said, "If what you tell is true, and it does seem reasonable, as you have said, then being so simple, if all people did it, there would not be enough wealth to go around."

"Wealth grows wherever people exert energy," Arkad replied. "If a rich man builds him a new palace, is the gold he pays out gone? No, the brickmaker has part of it, and the laborer has part of it, and the artist has part of it. And everyone who labors upon the house has part of it Yet when the palace is completed, is it not worth all it cost? And is the ground upon which it stands not worth more because it is there? And is the ground that adjoins it not worth more because it is there? Wealth grows in magic ways. No one can prophesy the limit of it. Have not the Phoenicians built great cities on barren coasts with the wealth that comes from their ships of commerce on the seas?"

"What then do you advise us to do that we also may become rich?" asked still another of his friends. "The years have passed and we are no longer young, and we have nothing put by."

"I advise that you take the wisdom of Algamish and say to yourselves, 'A part of all I earn is mine to keep.' Say it in the morning when you first arise. Say it at noon. Say it at night. Say it each hour of every day. Say it to yourself until the words stand out like letters of fire across the sky.

"Impress yourself with the idea. Fill yourself with the thought. Then take whatever portion seems wise. Let it be not less than one-tenth and lay it by. Arrange your other expenditures to do this if necessary. But lay by that portion first. Soon you will realize what a rich feeling it is to own a treasure upon which you alone have claim. As it grows it will stimulate you. A new joy of life will thrill you. Greater efforts will come to you to earn more. For of your increased earnings, will not the same percentage also be yours to keep?

"Then learn to make your treasure work for you. Make it your slave. Make its children and its children's children work for you.

"Ensure an income for your future. Look at the aged and forget not that in the days to come you also will be numbered among them. Therefore invest your treasure with greatest caution that it be not lost. Usurious rates of return are deceitful sirens that sing but to lure the unwary upon the rocks of loss and remorse.

"Provide also that your family may not want should the gods call you to their realms. For such protection it is always possible to make provision with small payments at regular intervals. Therefore the provident man delays not in expectation of a large sum becoming available for such a wise purpose.

"Counsel with those who are wise. Seek the advice of those whose daily work is handling money. Let them save you from such an error as I myself made in entrusting my money to the judgment of Azmur the brickmaker. A small return and a safe one is far more desirable than risk.

"Enjoy life while you are here. Do not overstrain or try to save too much. If one-tenth of all you earn is as much as you can comfortably keep, be content to keep this portion. Live otherwise according to your income, and let not yourself become stingy and afraid to spend. Life is good, and life is rich with things worthwhile and things to enjoy."

His friends thanked him and went away. Some were silent because they had no imagination and could not understand. Some were sarcastic because they thought that one so rich should divide his wealth with old friends not so fortunate. But some had in their eyes a new light. They realized that Algamish had come back each time to the room of the scribes because he was watching a man work his way out of darkness into light. When that man had found the light, a place awaited him. No one could fill that place until he had worked out for himself his own understanding, until he was ready for opportunity.

These latter were the ones who, in the following years, frequently revisited Arkad, who received them gladly. He counseled with them and gave them freely of his wisdom, as those of broad experience are always glad to do. And he assisted them in so investing their savings that it would bring in a good interest with safety and would neither be lost nor entangled in investments that paid no dividends.

The turning point in their lives came on that day when they realized the truth that had come from Algamish to Arkad and from Arkad to them:

A part of all you earn is yours to keep.

Seven Cures For a Lean Purse

The glory of Babylon endures. Down through the ages its reputation comes to us as the richest of cities, its treasures as fabulous.

Yet it was not always so. The riches of Babylon were the results of the wisdom of its people. They first had to learn how to become wealthy.

When the Good King, Sargon, returned to Babylon after defeating his enemies the Elamites, he was confronted with a serious situation. The Royal Chancellor explained it to the king thus:

"After many years of great prosperity—brought to our people because your majesty built the great irrigation canals and the mighty temples of the gods—now that these works are completed, the people seem unable to support themselves.

"The laborers are without employment. The merchants have few customers. The farmers are unable to sell their produce. The people have not enough gold to buy food."

"But where has all the gold gone that we spent for these great improvements?" demanded the king.

"It has found its way, I fear," responded the Chancellor, "into the possession of a few very rich men of our city. It filtered through the fingers of most our people as quickly as the goat's milk goes through the strainer. Now that the stream of gold has ceased to flow, most of our people have nothing to show for their earnings."

The king was thoughtful for some time. Then he asked, "Why should so few be able to acquire all the gold?"

"Because they know how," replied the Chancellor. "One may not condemn them for succeeding because they know how. Neither may one with justice take away what they have fairly earned, to give to others of less ability."

"But why," demanded the king, "should not all the people learn how to accumulate gold and therefore become themselves rich and prosperous?"

Quite possible, your excellency. But who can teach them? Certainly not the priests, because they know naught of money making."

"Who knows best in all our city how to become wealthy, Chancellor?" asked the king.

"Thy question answers itself, your majesty. Who has amassed the greatest wealth in Babylon?"

"Well said, my able Chancellor. It is Arkad. He is richest man in Babylon. Bring him before me on the morrow."

Upon the following day, as the king had decreed, Arkad appeared before him, straight and sprightly despite his three score years and ten.

"Arkad," spoke the king, "is it true you are the richest man in Babylon?"

"So it is reported, your majesty, and no one disputes it"

"How became you so wealthy?"

"By taking advantage of opportunities available to all citizens of our good city."

"You had nothing to start with?"

"Only a great desire for wealth. Besides this, nothing."

"Arkad," continued the king, "our city is in an unhappy state because a few know how to acquire wealth and therefore monopolize it, while the mass of our citizens lack the knowledge of how to keep any part of the gold they receive."

It is my desire that Babylon be the wealthiest city in the world. Therefore, it must be a city of many wealthy people. Therefore, we must teach all the people how to acquire riches. Tell me, Arkad, is there any secret to acquiring wealth? Can it be taught?"

"It is practical, your majesty. That which one person knows can be taught to others."

The king's eyes glowed. "Arkad, you speak the words I wish to hear. Will you lend yourself to this great cause? Will you teach your knowledge to a school for teachers, each of whom shall teach others until there are enough trained to teach these truths to every worthy subject in my domain?"

Arkad bowed and said, "I am your humble servant to command. Whatever knowledge I possess I will gladly give for the betterment of others and the glory of my king. Let your good chancellor arrange for me a class of one hundred students, and I will teach them those seven cures which did fatten my purse, than which there was none leaner in all of Babylon."

A fortnight later, in compliance with the king's command, the chosen hundred assembled in the great hall of the Temple of Learning, seated upon colorful rings in a semicircle. Arkad sat beside a small taboret upon which smoked a sacred lamp sending forth a strange and pleasing odor.

"Behold the richest man in Babylon," whispered a student, nudging his neighbor as Arkad arose. "He is but a man even as the rest of us."

"As a dutiful subject of our great king," Arkad began, "I stand before you in his service. Because I was once a poor youth who greatly desired gold, and because I found knowledge that enabled me to acquire it, he asks that I impart to you my knowledge.

"I started my fortune in the humblest way. I had no advantage not enjoyed as fully by you and every citizen in Babylon. "

The first storehouse of my treasure was a well-purse. I loathed its useless emptiness. I wanted it to be round and full, clinking with the sound of gold. Therefore, I sought every remedy for a lean purse. I found seven.

"To you assembled before me I shall explain the seven cures for a lean purse, which cures I do recommend to all who desire much gold. Each day for seven days I will explain to you one of the seven remedies.

"Listen attentively to the knowledge that I will impart. Debate it with me. Discuss it among yourselves. Learn these lessons thoroughly, that you may also plant in your own purse the seed of wealth. First each of you must start wisely to build a fortune of your own. Then will you be competent, and then only, to teach these truths to others.

"I shall teach you in simple ways how to fatten your purse. This is the first step leading to the temple of wealth, and no one may climb who cannot plant his feet firmly upon the first step.

"We shall now consider the first cure."

The First Cure: Start your purse to fattening

Arkad addressed a thoughtful man in the second row. "My good friend, at what craft do you work you?"

"I," replied the man, "am a scribe and carve records upon the clay tablets."

"Even at such labor did I myself earn my first coppers. Therefore, you have the same opportunity to build a fortune."

He spoke to a florid-faced man, farther back. "Pray tell also what you do to earn your bread?"

"I," responded this man, "am a meat butcher. I buy the goats the farmers raise, kill them, and sell the meat to the households and the hides to the sandal makers."

"Because you also labor and earn, you have every advantage to succeed that I possessed."

In this way Arkad proceeded to find out how each one labored to earn a living. When he had finished questioning them, he said:

"Now, my students, you can see that there are many trades and labors at which one may earn coins. Each of the ways of earning is a stream of gold from which the worker diverts a portion to his own purse. Therefore into the purse of each of you flows a stream of coins large or small according to your ability. Is it not so?"

Thereupon they agreed that it was so. "Then," continued Arkad, "if each of you desires to build for yourself a fortune, is it not wise to start by utilizing that source of wealth you have already established?"

To this they agreed.

Then Arkad turned to a humble man who had declared himself an egg merchant. "If you select one of your baskets and put into it each morning ten eggs, and take out from it each evening nine eggs, what will eventually happen?"

"It will, in time, become overflowing."

"Why?"

"Because each day I put in one more egg than I take out."

Arkad turned to the class with a smile. "Does anyone here have a lean purse?"

First they looked amused. Then they laughed. Lastly they waved their purses in jest.

"All right," he continued, "now I shall tell you the first remedy I learned to cure a lean purse. Do exactly as I have suggested to the egg merchant. For every ten coins you place within your purse, take out for use but nine. Your purse will start to fatten at once, and its increasing weight will feel good in your hand and bring satisfaction to your soul.

"Deride not what I say because of its simplicity. Truth is always simple. I told you I would tell how I built my fortune. This was my beginning. I, too, carried a lean purse and cursed it because there was nothing in it to satisfy my desires. But when I began to take out from my purse but nine parts of the ten I put in, it began to fatten. So will yours.

"Now I will tell a strange truth, the reason for which I know not. When I ceased to pay out more than nine-tenths of my earnings, I managed to get along just as well. I was not shorter than before. Also, before long, coins came to me more easily than before. Surely it is a law of the gods that unto those who keep (and spend not) a certain part of all their earnings, shall gold come more easily. Likewise, those whose purse is empty does gold avoid.

"Which do you desire the most? Is it the gratification of your desires of each day: a jewel, a bit of finery, better raiment, more food; things quickly gone and forgotten? Or is it substantial belongings: gold, lands, herds, merchandise, income-bringing investments? The coins you take from your purse bring the first. The coins you leave within it will bring the latter.

"This, my students, was the first cure I discovered for my lean purse: 'For each ten coins I put in, to spend but nine.' Debate this among yourselves. If any of you proves it untrue, tell me upon the morrow when we shall meet again."

The Second Cure: Control your expenditures

"Some of your members, my students, have asked me this: How can we keep one-tenth of all we earn when all the coins we earn are not enough for our necessary expenses?" So did Arkad address his students upon the second day.

"Yesterday how many of you carried lean purses?"

"All of us," answered the class.

"Yet you do not all earn the same. Some earn much more than others. Some have much larger families to support. Yet all purses were equally lean. Now I will tell you an unusual truth: What each of us calls our 'necessary expenses' will always grow to equal our incomes unless we protest to the contrary.

"Confuse not necessary expenses with your desires. Each of you, together with your good families, have more desires than your earnings can gratify. Therefore your earnings are spent to gratify these desires, insofar as they will go. Still you retain many ungratified desires.

"All people are burdened with more desires than they can gratify. Because of my wealth do you think I may gratify every desire? 'Tis a false idea. There are limits to my time. There are limits to my strength. There are limits to the distance I may travel. There are limits to what I may eat. There are limits to the zest with which I may enjoy.

"I say to you that just as weeds grow in a field wherever the farmer leaves space for their roots, even so freely do desires grow in us whenever there is a possibility of their being gratified. Our desires are a multitude, and those that we may gratify are but few.

"Study thoughtfully your accustomed habits of living. Herein may be most often found certain accepted expenses that may be wisely reduced or eliminated. Let your motto be one hundred percent of appreciated value demanded for each coin spent.

"Therefore, engrave upon the clay each thing for which you desire to spend. Select those that are necessary and others that are possible through the expenditure of nine-tenths of your income. Cross out the rest and consider them but a part of that great multitude of desires that must go unsatisfied, and regret them not.

"Then budget your necessary expenses. Touch not the one-tenth that is fattening your purse. Let this be your great desire that is being fulfilled. Keep working with your budget, keep adjusting it to help you. Make it your first assistant in defending your fattening purse."

Hereupon one of the students, wearing a robe of red and gold, arose and said, "I am a free man. I believe that it is my right to enjoy the good things of life. Therefore do I rebel against the slavery of a budget which determines just how much I may spend and for what. I feel it would take much pleasure from my life and make me little more than a pack-ass to carry a burden."

To him Arkad replied, "Who, my friend, would determine your budget?"

"I would make it for myself," responded the protesting one.

"In that case, were a pack-ass to budget his burden, would he include therein jewels and rugs and heavy bars of gold? Not so. He would include hay and grain and a bag of water for the desert trail.

"The purpose of a budget is to help your purse to fatten. It is to assist you to have your necessities and, insofar as attainable, your other desires. It is to enable you to realize your most cherished wishes by defending them from your casual wants. Like a bright light in a dark cave, your budget shows up the leaks from your purse and enables you to stop them and control your expenditures for definite and gratifying purposes.

"This, then, is the second cure for a lean purse: *Budget your expenses that you may have coins to pay for your necessities, to pay for your enjoyments, and to gratify your worthwhile desires without spending more than nine-tenths of your earnings.*"

The Third Cure: Make your gold multiply

"Behold, your lean purse is fattening. You have disciplined yourself to leave therein one-tenth of all that you earn. You have controlled your expenditures to protect your growing treasure. Next, we will consider means to put your treasure to labor and to increase. Gold in a purse is gratifying to own and satisfies a miserly soul, but it earns nothing. The gold we may retain from our earnings is but the start. The earnings it will make shall build our fortunes." So spoke Arkad upon the third day to his class.

"How therefore may we put our gold to work? My first investment was unfortunate, for I lost it all. Its tale I will relate later. My first profitable investment was a loan I made to a man named Aggar, a shield maker. Once each year he bought large shipments of bronze from across the sea to use in his trade. Lacking sufficient capital to pay the merchants, he would borrow from those who had extra coins. He was an honorable man. His borrowing he would repay, together with a liberal rental, as he sold his shields.

"Each time I loaned to him, I loaned back also the rental he had paid to me. Therefore not only did my capital increase, but its earnings likewise increased. Most gratifying it was to have these sums return to my purse.

"I tell you, my students, our wealth is not in the coins we carry in our purse; it is the income we build, the golden stream that continually flows into our purse and keeps it always bulging. That is what every person desires. That is what you, each one of you desires: an income that continues to come whether you work or travel.

"Great income I have acquired—so great that I am called a very rich man. My loans to Aggar were my first training in profitable investment. Gaining wisdom from this experience, I extended my loans and investments as my capital increased. From a few sources at first, from many sources later, flowed into my purse a golden stream of wealth available for such wise uses as I should decide.

"Behold, from my humble earnings I had begotten a hoard of golden slaves, each laboring and earning more gold. As they labored for me, so their children also labored, and their children's children, until great was the income from their combined efforts.

"Gold increases rapidly when making reasonable earnings, as you will see from the following: A farmer, when his first son was born, took ten pieces of silver to a money lender and asked him to keep it on rental for his son until he became twenty years of age. This the money lender did, and agreed the rental should be one-fourth of its value each four years. The farmer asked, because this sum he had set aside as belonging to his son, that the rental be add to the principal.

"When the boy had reached the age of twenty years, the farmer again went to the money lender to inquire about the silver. The money lender explained that because this sum had been increased by compound interest, the original ten pieces of silver had now grown to thirty and one-half pieces.

"The farmer was well pleased, and because the son did not need the coins, he left them with the money lender. When the son became fifty years of age, the father meantime having passed to the other world, the money lender paid the son in settlement one hundred and sixty-seven pieces of silver.

"Thus in fifty years had the investment multiplied itself at rental almost seventeen times.

"This, then, is the third cure for a lean purse: to put each coin to laboring that it may reproduce its kind, even as the flocks of the field, and help bring to you income, a stream of wealth that shall flow constantly into your purse."

The Fourth Cure: Guard your treasures from loss

"Misfortune loves a shining mark. Gold in one's purse must be guarded with firmness else it be lost. Thus it is wise that we must first secure small amounts and learn to protect them before the gods entrust us with larger." So spoke Arkad upon the fourth day to his class.

"Every owner of gold is tempted by opportunities whereby it would seem possible to make large sums by its investment in most plausible projects. Often friends and relatives are eagerly entering such investment and urge him to follow.

"The first sound principle of investment is security for your principal. Is it wise to be intrigued by larger earnings when your principal may be lost? I say not. The penalty of risk is probable loss. Study carefully, before parting with your treasure, each assurance that it may be safely reclaimed. Be not misled by your own romantic desires to make wealth rapidly.

"Before you loan it to anyone, assure yourself of the person's ability to repay and reputation for doing so, that you may not unwittingly be giving away your hard-earned treasure.

"Before you entrust it as an investment in any field, acquaint yourself with the dangers which may beset it.

"My own first investment was a tragedy to me at the time. The guarded savings of a year I entrusted to a brickmaker, named Azmur, who was traveling over the far seas and agreed to buy for me in Tyre the rare jewels of the Phoenicians. These we would sell upon his return and divide the profits. The Phoenicians were scoundrels and sold him bits of glass. My treasure was lost. Today, my training would show to me at once the folly of entrusting a brickmaker to buy jewels.

"Therefore I advise you from the wisdom of my experiences: be not too confident of your own wisdom in entrusting your treasures to the possible pitfalls of investments. Better by far to consult the wisdom of those experienced in handling money for profit. Such advice is freely given for the asking and may readily possess a value equal in gold to the sum you consider investing. In truth, such is its actual value if it save you from loss.

"This, then, is the fourth cure for a lean purse, and of great importance if it prevent your purse from being emptied once it has become well filled: *Guard your treasure from loss by investing only where your principal is safe, where it may be reclaimed if desirable, and where you will not fail to collect a fair rental. Consult with those who are wise. Secure the advice of those experienced in the profitable handling of gold. Let their wisdom protect your treasure from unsafe investments.*"

The Fifth Cure: Make of your dwelling a profitable investment

"If you set aside nine parts of your earnings upon which to live and enjoy life, and if you can turn any of this nine parts into a profitable investment without detriment to your well-being, then so much faster will your treasure grow." So spoke Arkad to his class at their fifth lesson.

"All too many of those in Babylon raise their families in unseemly quarters. They pay to exacting landlords liberal rentals for rooms where they have not a spot to raise the blooms that gladden the heart, and their children have no place to play except in the unclean alleys.

"No family can fully enjoy life unless they have a plot of ground wherein children can play in the clean earth and where they may raise not only blossoms but good, rich herbs to eat.

"It brings gladness to eat the figs from your own trees and the grapes of your own vines. To own your domicile, and have it a place you are proud to care for, puts confidence in your heart and greater effort behind all your endeavors. Therefore, I recommend that every family own the roof that shelters them.

"Nor is it beyond the ability of any family to own their home. Has not our great king so widely extended the walls of Babylon that within them much land is now unused and may be purchased at sums most reasonable?

"Also I say to you, my students, that the money lenders gladly consider the desires of those who seek homes and land for their families. Readily may you borrow to pay the brickmaker and the builder for such commendable purposes, if you can show a reasonable portion of the necessary sum which you yourself have provided for the purpose.

"Then when the house is built, you can pay the money lender with the same regularity as you did pay the landlord. Because each payment will reduce your indebtedness to the money lender, a few years will satisfy the loan.

"Then will your heart be glad because you will own in your own right a valuable property, and your only cost will be the king's taxes.

"Thus come many blessings to those who own their own house. And greatly will it reduce their cost of living, making available more of their earnings for pleasures and the gratification of their desires. This, then, is the fifth cure for a lean purse: *Own your own home*"

The Sixth Cure: Insure a future income

"The life of every person proceeds from childhood to old age. This is the path of life, and no one may deviate from it unless the gods call them prematurely to the world beyond. Therefore do I say that it behooves us all to make preparation for a suitable income in the days to come, when we are no longer young, and to make preparations for our family should we be no longer with them to comfort and support them. This lesson shall instruct you in providing a full purse when time has made you less able to learn." So Arkad addressed his class upon the sixth day.

"Those who, because of their understanding of the laws of wealth, acquire a growing surplus should give thought to those future days. They should plan certain investments or provision that may endure safely for many years, yet will be available when the time arrives which they have so wisely anticipated.

"There are many ways by which you may provide with safety for your future. You may provide a hiding place and there bury a secret treasure. Yet, no matter with what skill it be hidden, it may nevertheless become the loot of thieves. For this reason I recommend not this plan.

"You may buy houses or lands for this purpose. If wisely chosen as to their usefulness and value in the future, they are permanent in their value, and their earnings or their sale will provide well for your purpose.

"You may loan a small sum to the money lender and increase it at regular periods. The rental which the money lender adds to this will largely add to its increase. I know a sandal maker, named Ansan, who explained to me not long ago that each week for eight years he deposited with his money lender two pieces of silver. The money lender had but recently given him an accounting over which he greatly rejoiced. The total of his small deposits, with their rental at the customary rate of one-fourth their value for each four years, had now become a thousand and forty pieces of silver.

"I gladly encouraged him further by demonstrating to him with my knowledge of the numbers that in twelve years more, if he would keep his regular deposits of but two pieces of silver each week, the money lender would then owe him four thousand pieces of silver, a worthy competence for the rest of his life.

"Surely, when such a small payment made with regularity produces such profitable results, no one can afford not to insure a treasure for their old age and the protection of their family, no matter how prosperous their business and investments may be.

"I would that I might say more about this. In my mind rests a belief that someday the wise will devise a plan to insure against death, whereby many pay in but a trifling sum regularly, the aggregate making a handsome sum for the family of each member who passes to the beyond. This I see as something desirable and which I could highly recommend.

But today it is not possible, because it must reach beyond the life of any person or any partnership to operate. It must be as stable as the king's throne. I feel that someday such a plan shall come to pass and be a great blessing to many, because even the first small payment will make available a snug fortune for the family of a member who passes on.

"But because we live in our own day and not in the days to come, we must take advantage of those means and ways of accomplishing our purposes. Therefore I recommend to all that they, by wise and well-thought-out methods, provide against a lean purse in their mature years. To do otherwise is a sore tragedy.

"This, then, is the sixth cure for a lean purse: *Provide in advance for the needs of your growing age and the protection of your family.*"

The Seventh Cure: Increase your ability to earn

"This day I speak to you, my students, of one of the most vital remedies for a lean purse. Yet I will talk not of gold but of yourselves, those beneath the robes of many colors who sit before me. I will talk to you of those things within the minds and lives of many which work for or against their success." So did Arkad address his class upon the seventh day.

"Not long ago a young man came to me seeking to borrow. When I asked him the cause of his necessity, he complained that his earnings were insufficient to pay his expenses. Thereupon I explained to him, this being the case, that he was a poor customer for the money lender, as he possessed no surplus earning capacity to repay the loan.

"'What you need, young man,' I told him, 'is to earn more coins. How do you increase your capacity to earn?'

"'All that I can do' he replied. 'Six times within two moons I have approached my master to request that my pay be increased, but without success. No one can go oftener than that.'

"We may smile at his simplicity, yet he possessed one of the vital requirements to increase his earnings. Within him was a strong desire to earn more, a proper and commendable desire.

"*Preceding accomplishment must be desire. Your desires must be strong and definite.* General desires are but weak longings. To wish to be rich is of little purpose. To desire five pieces of gold is a tangible desire which you can press to fulfillment. After you have backed your desire for five pieces of gold with strength of purpose to secure it, next you can find similar ways to obtain ten pieces, and then twenty pieces, and later a thousand pieces, and, behold, you have become wealthy. In learning to secure one definite small desire, you have trained yourself to secure a larger one. This is the process by which wealth is accumulated: first in small sums, then in larger ones as you learn and become more capable.

"Desires must be simple and definite. They defeat their own purpose should they be too many, too confusing, or beyond one's training to accomplish. "

As you perfect yourself in your calling, even so does your ability to earn increase. When I was a humble scribe carving upon the clay for a few coppers each day, I observed that other workers did more than I and were paid more. Therefore I determined that I would be exceeded by none. Nor did it take long for me to discover the reason for their greater success. More interest in my work, more concentration upon my task, more persistence in my effort, and, behold, few could carve more tablets in a day than I. With reasonable promptness my increased skill was rewarded, nor was it necessary for me to go six times to my master to request recognition.

"The more of wisdom we know, the more we may earn. Those who seek to learn more of their craft shall be richly rewarded. If you are an artisan, you may seek to learn the methods and tools of those most skillful in the same line. If you labor at the law or at healing, you may consult and exchange knowledge with others of your calling. If you be a merchant, you may continually seek better goods that can be purchased at lower prices.

"Always do human affairs change and improve because those who are keen-minded seek greater skill that they may better serve those upon whose patronage they depend. Therefore, I urge all of you to be in the front rank of progress and not to stand still, lest you be left behind.

"Many things come to make life rich with gainful experiences. Such things as the following you must do if you respect yourself:

"*You must pay your debts with all the promptness within your power, not purchasing that for which you are unable to pay.*

"You must take care of your family that they may think and speak well of you.

"You must make a will of record that, in case the gods call you, proper and honorable division of your property may be accomplished.

"You must have compassion upon those who are injured and smitten by misfortune and aid them within reasonable limits. You must do deeds of thoughtfulness to those dear to you.

"Thus, the seventh and last remedy for a lean purse is to cultivate your own powers, to study and become wiser, to become more skillful, to so act as to respect yourself. Thereby you shall acquire confidence in yourself to achieve your carefully considered desires.

"These, then, are the seven cures for a lean purse, which, out of the experience of a long and successful life, I urge for all who desire wealth.

"There is more gold in Babylon, my students, than you dream of. There is abundance for all.

"Go forth and practice these truths, that you may prosper and grow wealthy, as is your right.

"Go forth and teach these truths, that every honorable subject of our king may also share liberally in the ample wealth of our beloved city."

Meet the Goddess of Good Luck

"If a man be lucky, there is no foretelling the possible extent of his good fortune. Pitch him into the Euphrates„ and like as not he will swim out with a pearl in his hand."

—Babylonian Proverb.

The desire to be lucky is universal. It was just as strong in those who lived four thousand years ago in ancient Babylon as it is in the hearts of people today. We all hope to be favored by the whimsical Goddess of Good Luck.

Is there some way we can meet her and attract, not only her favorable attention but her generous favors? Is there a way to attract good luck?

That is just what the inhabitants of ancient Babylon wished to know. It is exactly what they decided to find out. They were shrewd and keen thinkers. That explains why their city became the richest and most powerful city of their time.

In that distant past, they had no schools or colleges. Nevertheless, they had a center of learning, and a very practical one it was. Among the towered buildings in Babylon was one that ranked in importance with the palace of the king, the hanging gardens, and the temples of the gods. You will find scant mention of it in the history books, more likely no mention at all, yet it exerted a powerful influence upon the thought of that time.

This building was the Temple of Learning, where the wisdom of the past was expounded by voluntary teachers, and where subjects of popular interest were discussed in open forums. Within its walls all met as equals. The humblest of slaves could dispute with impunity the opinions of a prince of the royal house.

Among the many who frequented the Temple of Learning was a wise, rich man named Arkad, called the richest man in Babylon. He had his own special hall where almost any evening a large group of people, some old, some very young, but mostly middle-aged, gathered to discuss and argue interesting subjects. Suppose we listen in to see whether they knew how to attract good luck.

The sun had just set like a great red ball of fire shining through the haze of desert dust when Arkad strolled to his accustomed platform. Already full fourscore listeners were awaiting his arrival, reclining on their small rugs spread upon the floor. More were still arriving.

"What shall we discuss this night?" Arkad inquired.

After a brief hesitation, a tall cloth weaver addressed him, arising as was the custom. "I have a subject I would like to hear discussed yet hesitate to offer lest it seem ridiculous to you, Arkad, and my good friends here."

Upon being urged to offer it, both by Arkad and by calls from the others, he continued: "This day I have been lucky, for I have found a purse in which there are pieces of gold. To continue to be lucky is my great desire. Feeling that all here share with me this desire, I suggest we debate how to attract good luck that we may discover ways it can be enticed to one."

"A most interesting subject has been offered," Arkad commented, "one most worthy of our discussion. To some, good luck is but a chance happening that, like an accident, may befall one without purpose or reason. Others believe that the instigator of all good fortune is our most bounteous goddess, Ashtar, ever anxious to reward with generous gifts those who please her. Speak up, my friends, what say you? Shall we seek to find if there be means by which good luck may be enticed to visit each and all of us?"

"Yea! Yea! And much of it!" responded the growing group of eager listeners.

Thereupon Arkad continued, "To start our discussion, let us first hear from those among us who have enjoyed experiences similar to that of the cloth weaver in finding or receiving, without effort upon their part, valuable treasures or jewels."

There was a pause in which all looked about expecting someone to reply, but no one did.

"What, no one?" Arkad said. "Then rare indeed must be this kind of good luck. Who now will offer a suggestion as to where we shall continue our search?"

"That I will do," spoke a well-robed young man, arising. "When one such as I speak of luck, is it not natural that his thoughts turn to the gaining tables? Is it not there we find many courting the favor of the goddess in hope she will bless them with rich winnings?"

As he resumed his seat a voice called, "Do not stop! Continue your story! Tell us, did you find favor with the goddess at the gaming tables? Did she turn the cubes with red side up so you filled your purse at the dealer's expense, or did she permit the blue sides to come up so the dealer raked in your hard-earned pieces of silver?"

The young man joined the good-natured laughter, then replied, "I am not averse to admitting she seemed not to know I was even there. But how about the rest of you? Have you found her waiting about such places to roll the cubes in your favor? We are eager to hear as well as to learn."

"A wise start," broke in Arkad. "We meet here to consider all sides of each question. To ignore the gaming table would be to overlook an instinct common to most people, the love of taking a chance with a small amount of silver in the hope of winning much gold."

"That reminds me of the races but yesterday," called out another listener. "If the goddess frequents the gaming tables, certainly she does not overlook the races where the gilded chariots and the foaming horses offer far more excitement. Tell us honestly, Arkad, did she whisper to you to place your bet upon those gray horses from Nineveh yesterday? I was standing just behind you and could scarce believe my ears when I heard you place your bet upon the grays. You know as well as any that no team in all Assyria can beat our beloved bays in a fair race.

"Did the goddess whisper in your ear to bet upon the grays because at the last turn the inside black would stumble and so interfere with our bays that the grays would win the race and score an unearned victory?"

Arkad smiled indulgently at the banter. "What reason have we to feel that the good goddess would take that much interest in anyone's bet upon a horse race? To me she is a goddess of love and dignity whose pleasure it is to aid those who are in need and to reward those who are deserving. I look to find her, not at the gaming tables or the races where fools lose more gold than they win, but in other places where the activities are more worthwhile and more worthy of reward.

"In tilling the soil, in honest trading, in all occupations, there is opportunity to make a profit upon our efforts and our transactions. Perhaps not all the time will we be rewarded, because sometimes our judgment may be faulty and other times the winds and the weather may defeat our efforts. Yet, if we persist, we may usually expect to realize a profit. This is so because, in such activities, the chances of profit are always in our favor.

"But, when we play the games, the situation is reversed, for the chances of profit are always against us and always in favor of the game keepers. The game is so arranged that it will always favor the keepers. It is their business at which they plan to make a liberal profit from the coins bet by the players. Few players realize how certain are the game keeper's profits and how uncertain are their own chances to win.

"For example, let us consider wagers placed upon the cube. Each time it is cast, we bet which side will be uppermost. If it be the red side, the game master pays to us four times our bet. But if any other of the five sides come uppermost, we lose our bet. Thus the figures show that for each cast we have five chances to lose, but because the red pays four for one, we have four chances to win. In a night's play, the game master can expect to keep for his profit one-fifth of all the coins wagered. Can we expect to win more than occasionally against odds so arranged that we should lose one-fifth of all our bets?"

"Yet some do win large sums at times," volunteered one of the listeners.

"Quite so, they do," Arkad continued. "Realizing this, the question comes to me whether money secured in such ways brings permanent value to those who are thus lucky. Among my acquaintances are many of the successful inhabitants of Babylon, yet among them I am unable to name any who started their success from such a source.

"You who are gathered here tonight know many more of our substantial citizens. To me it would be of much interest to learn how many of them can credit the gaming tables with their start to success. Suppose each of you tell of those you know. What say you?"

After a prolonged silence, a wag ventured, 'Would your inquiry include the game keepers?"

"If you think of no one else," Arkad responded. "If not one of you can think of anyone else, then how about yourselves? Are there any consistent winners with us who hesitate to advise such a source for their incomes?"

His challenge was answered by a series of groans from the rear, taken up and spread amid much laughter.

"It would seem we are not seeking good luck in such places as the goddess frequents," he continued. "Therefore let us explore other fields. We have not found it in picking up lost wallets. Neither have we found it haunting the gaming tables. As to the races, I must confess to having lost far more coins there than I have ever won.

"Now, suppose we consider our trades and businesses. Is it not natural if we conclude a profitable transaction to consider it not good luck but a just reward for our efforts? I am inclined to think we may be overlooking the gifts of the goddess. Perhaps she really does assist us when we do not appreciate her generosity. Who can suggest further discussion?"

Thereupon an elderly merchant arose, smoothing his genteel white robe. "With your permission, most honorable Arkad and my friends, I offer a suggestion. If, as you have said, we take credit to our own industry and ability for our business success, why not consider the successes we almost enjoyed but which escaped us, happenings which would have been most profitable. They would have been rare examples of good luck if they had actually happened. Because they were not brought to fulfillment, we cannot consider them as our just rewards. Surely many here have such experiences to relate."

"Here is a wise approach," Arkad approved. "Who among you have had good luck within your grasp only to see it escape?"

Many hands were raised, among them that of the merchant. Arkad motioned to him to speak. "As you suggested this approach, we should like to hear first from you."

"I will gladly relate a tale," he resumed, "that shows how closely good luck may approach and how blindly we may permit it to escape, much to our loss and later regret.

"Many years ago, when I was a young man, just married and well-started to earning, my father came one day and urged most strongly that I enter into an investment. The son of one of his good friends had taken notice of a barren tract of land not far beyond the outer walls of our city. It lay high above the canal where no water could reach it.

"The son of my father's friend devised a plan to purchase this land, build three large water wheels that could be operated by oxen, and thereby raise the life-giving waters to the fertile soil. This accomplished, he planned to divide into small tracts and sell to the residents of the city for herb patches.

"The son of my father's friend did not possess sufficient gold to complete such an undertaking. Like myself, he was a young man earning a fair sum. His father, like mine, was a man of large family and small means. He, therefore, decided to interest a group of investors to enter the enterprise with him. The group was to comprise twelve, all of whom must be money earners and agree to pay one-tenth of their earnings into the enterprise until the land was made ready for sale. All would then share justly in the profits in proportion to their investment. "

'You, my son,' spoke my father unto me, 'are now in your young manhood. It is my deep desire that you begin the building of a valuable estate for myself that you may become respected among your peers. I desire to see you profit from a knowledge of the thoughtless mistakes of your father.'

"'This I most ardently desire, my father,' I replied.

"'Then this I advise: do what I should have done at your age. From your earnings keep out one-tenth to put into favorable investments. With this one-tenth of your earnings and what it will also earn, you can, before you are my age, accumulate for yourself a valuable estate.'

"'These are words of wisdom, my father. I greatly desire riches. Yet there are many uses to which my earnings are called. Therefore, I hesitate to do as you advise. I am young. There is plenty of time.'

"'So I thought at your age; yet behold, many years have passed, and I have not yet made the beginning.'

"'We live in a different age, my father. I shall avoid your mistakes.'

"'Opportunity stands before you, my son. It is offering a chance that may lead to wealth. I beg of you, do not delay. Go upon the morrow to the son of my friend and bargain with him to pay ten percent of your earnings into this investment. Go promptly upon the morrow. Opportunity waits for no one. Today it is here; soon it is gone. Therefore, delay not!'

"In spite of the advice of my father, I hesitated. There were beautiful new robes just brought by the tradesmen from the East, robes of such richness and beauty my good wife and I felt we must each possess one. Should I agree to pay one-tenth of my earnings into the enterprise, we must deprive ourselves of these and other pleasures we dearly desired. I delayed making a decision until it was too late, much to my subsequent regret. The enterprise proved to be more profitable than anyone had prophesied. This is my tale, showing how I allowed good luck to escape."

"In this tale we see how good luck waits to come to those who accept opportunity," commented a swarthy man of the desert. "To the building of an estate there must always be the beginning. That start may be a few pieces of gold or silver which we divert from our earnings to our first investment. I, myself, am the owner of many herds. The start of my herds I began when I was a mere boy and purchased with one piece of silver a young calf. This, being the beginning of my wealth, was of great importance to me.

"To take his first start to building an estate is as good luck as can come to anyone. With all of us, that first step, which changes us from those who earn from their own labor to those who draw dividends from the earnings of their gold, is important. Some, fortunately, take it when young and thereby outstrip in financial success those who take it later or those unfortunates, like the father of this merchant, who never take it.

"Had our friend, the merchant, taken this step in his early manhood when this opportunity came to him, this day he would be blessed with much more of this world's goods. Should the good luck of our friend, the cloth weaver, cause him to take such a step at this time, it will indeed be but the beginning of much greater good fortune."

"Thank you! I like to speak, also." A stranger from another country arose. "I am a Syrian. Not so well do I speak your tongue. I wish to call this friend, the merchant, a name. Maybe you think it not polite, this name. Yet I wish to call him that. But, alas, I not know your word for it. If I call it in Syrian, you will not understand. Therefore, please some good gentlemen, tell me that right name you call those who put off doing those things that mighty good for them."

"Procrastinators," called a voice.

"That's him," shouted the Syrian, waving his hands excitedly, "he accepts not opportunity when she comes. He waits. He says I have much business right now. Bye and bye I talk to you. Opportunity, she will not wait for such slow fellow. She thinks if we desires to be lucky we will step quick. Those who not step quick when opportunity comes, they big procrastinators like our friend, this merchant."

The merchant arose and bowed good-naturedly in response to

the laughter. "My admiration to you, stranger within our gates, who hesitates not to speak the truth."

"And now let us hear another tale of opportunity. Who has for us another experience?" demanded Arkad.

"I have," responded a red-robed man of middle age. "I am a buyer of animals, mostly camels and horses. Sometimes I also buy the sheep and goats. The tale I am about to relate will tell truthfully how opportunity came one night when I least expected it. Perhaps for this reason I let it escape. Of this you shall be the judge.

"Returning to the city one evening after a disheartening ten-days' journey in search of camels, I was much angered to find the gates of the city closed and locked. While my slaves spread our tent for the night, which we looked to spend with little food and no I water, I was approached by an elderly farmer who, like ourselves, found himself locked outside.

"'Honored sir,' he addressed me, 'from your appearance, I judge you to be a buyer. If this be so, I would like to sell to you the most excellent flock of sheep just driven up. Alas, my good wife lies very sick with the fever. I must return with all haste. Buy my sheep that I and my slaves may mount our camels and travel back without delay.'

"So dark it was that I could not see his flock, but from the bleating I knew it must be large. Having wasted ten days searching for camels I could not find, I was glad to bargain with him. In his anxiety, he set a most reasonable price. I accepted, well knowing my slaves could drive the flock through the city gates in the morning and sell at a substantial profit.

The bargain concluded, I called my slaves to bring torches that we might count the flock which the farmer declared to contain nine hundred. I shall not burden you, my friends, with a description of our difficulty in attempting to count so many thirsty, restless, milling sheep. It proved to be an impossible task. Therefore, I bluntly informed the farmer I would count them at daylight and pay him then.

"'Please, most honorable sir,' he pleaded, 'pay me but two-thirds of the price tonight that I may be on my way. I will leave my most intelligent and educated slave to help make the count in the morning. He is trustworthy, and to him you can pay the balance.'

' "But I was stubborn and refused to make payment that night. Next morning, before I awoke, the city gates opened and four buyers rushed out in search of flocks. They were most eager and willing to pay high prices because the city was threatened with siege, and food was not plentiful. Nearly three times the price at which he had offered the flock to me did the old farmer receive for it. Thus was rare good luck allowed to escape."

"Here is a tale most unusual," commented Arkad. "What wisdom does it suggest?"

"The wisdom of making a payment immediately when we are convinced our bargain is wise," suggested a venerable saddle maker. "If the bargain be good, then we need protection against our own weaknesses as much as against anyone else. We mortals are changeable—alas, I must say more apt to change our minds when right than wrong. Wrong, we are stubborn indeed. Right, we are prone to vacillate and let opportunity escape. My first judgment is my best. Yet always have I found it difficult to compel myself to proceed with a good bargain when made. Therefore, as a protection against my own weaknesses, I make a prompt deposit thereon. This saves me from later regrets for the good luck that should have been mine."

"Thank you! Again I like to speak." The Syrian was upon his feet once more. "These tales much alike. Each time opportunity fly away for same reason. Each time she come to procrastinators, bringing good plan. Each time they hesitate, not say, right now best time, I do it quick. How can they succeed that way?"

"Wise are your words, my friend," responded the buyer. "Good luck fled from procrastination in both these tales. Yet this is not unusual. The spirit of procrastination is within all of us. We desire riches; yet, how often when opportunity appears before us, that spirit of procrastination from within urges various delays in our acceptance.

In listening to it we become our own worst enemies. "In my younger days I did not know it by this long word our friend from Syria enjoys. I thought at first it was my own poor judgment that caused me loss of many profitable trades. Later, I credited the problem to my stubborn disposition. At last, I recognized it for what it was—a habit of needless delaying where action was required, action prompt and decisive. How I hated it when its true character stood revealed. With the bitterness of a wild ass hitched to a chariot, I broke loose from this enemy to my success."

"Thank you! I like ask question from Mr. Merchant." The Syrian was speaking. "You wear fine robes, not like those of the poor. You speak like successful man. Tell us, do you listen now when procrastination whispers in your ear?"

"Like our friend the buyer, I also had to recognize and conquer procrastination," responded the merchant. "To me, it proved to be an enemy, ever watching and waiting to thwart my accomplishments. The tale I related is but one of many similar instances I could tell to show how it drove away my opportunities. 'Tis not difficult to conquer, once understood. No one willingly permits the thief to rob their bins of grain. Nor does anyone willingly permit an enemy to drive away customers and steal profits. When once I recognized that such acts as these my enemy was committing, with determination I conquered him. So must all master their own spirit of procrastination before they can expect to share in the rich treasures of Babylon.

"What say, Arkad? Because you are the richest man in Babylon, many proclaim you to be the luckiest. Do you agree with me that none can arrive at a full measure of success until they have completely crushed the spirit of procrastination within them?"

"It is even as you say," Arkad admitted. "During my long life I have watched generation following generation, marching forward along those avenues of trade, science and learning that lead to success in life. Opportunities came to them all. Some grasped theirs and moved steadily to the gratification of their deepest desires, but the majority hesitated, faltered, and fell behind."

Arkad turned to the cloth weaver. You suggested that we debate good luck. Let us now hear what you think upon the subject."

"I see good luck in a different light. I had thought of it as something most desirable that might happen to us without effort upon our parts. Now, I realize such happenings are not the sort of thing we may attract to ourselves. From our discussion I have learned that to attract good luck, it is necessary to take advantage of opportunities. Therefore, in the future, I shall endeavor to make the best of the opportunities that come to me."

"You have well grasped the truths brought forth in our discussion," Arkad replied. "Good luck, we do find, often follows opportunity but seldom comes otherwise. Our merchant friend would have found great good luck had he accepted the opportunity the good goddess did present to him. Our friend the buyer, likewise, would have enjoyed good luck had he completed the purchase of the flock and sold at such a handsome profit.

"We pursued this discussion to find a means by which good luck could be enticed to us. I feel that we have found the way. Both the tales showed how good luck follows opportunity. Herein lies a truth that many similar tales of good luck, won or lost, could not change. The truth is this: Good luck can be enticed by accepting opportunity.

"Those eager to grasp opportunities for their betterment attract the interest of the good goddess. She is ever anxious to aid those who please her. People of action please her best.

"Action will lead you forward to the successes you desire."

People of action are favored by the goddess of good luck.

The Five Laws of Gold

"A bag heavy with gold, or a clay tablet carved with words of wisdom: if you had your choice, which would you choose?"

By the flickering light from the fire of desert shrubs, the sun-tanned faces of the listeners gleamed with interest.

"The gold, the gold," chorused the twenty-seven.

Old Kalabab smiled knowingly.

"Hark," he resumed, raising his hand. "Hear the wild dogs out there in the night. They howl and wail because they are lean with hunger. Yet feed them, and what do they? Fight and strut. Then fight and strut some more, giving no thought to the morrow that will surely come.

"Just so it is with us. Give us a choice of gold and wisdom—what do we do? Ignore the wisdom and waste the gold. On the morrow we wail because we have no more gold.

"Gold is reserved for those who know its laws and abide by them."

Kalabab drew his white robe close about his lean legs, for a cool night wind was blowing.

"Because you have served me faithfully upon our long journey, because you cared well for my camels, because you toiled uncomplainingly across the hot sands of the desert, because you fought bravely the robbers that sought to despoil my merchandise, I will tell you this night the tale of the five laws of gold—such a tale as you never heard before.

"Hark you, with deep attention to the words I speak, for if you grasp their meaning and heed them, in the days that come you shall have much gold."

He paused impressively. Above, in a canopy of blue, the stars shone brightly in the crystal clear skies of Babylonia. Behind the group loomed their faded tents tightly staked against possible desert storms. Beside the tents were neatly stacked bales of merchandise covered with skins. Nearby the camel herd sprawled in the sand, some chewing their cuds contentedly, others snoring in hoarse discord.

"You have told us many good tales, Kalabab," spoke up the chief packer. "We look to your wisdom to guide us upon the morrow when our service with you shall be at an end."

"I have but told you of my adventures in strange and distant lands, but this night I shall tell you of the wisdom of Arkad, the wise rich man."

"Much have we heard of him," acknowledged the chief packer, "for he was the richest man that ever lived in Babylon."

"The richest man he was, and that because be was wise in the ways of gold, even as no man had ever been before him. This night shall I tell you of his great wisdom as it was told to me by Nomasir, his son, many years ago in Nineveh, when I was but a lad.

"My master and myself had tarried long into the night in the palace of Nomasir. I had helped my master bring great bundles of fine rugs, each one to be tried by Nomasir until his choice of colors was satisfied. At last he was well pleased and commanded us to sit with him and to drink a rare vintage pleasant to the nostrils and most warming to my stomach, which was unaccustomed to such a drink.

"Then, he told us this tale of the great wisdom of Arkad, his father, even as I shall tell it to you.

"In Babylon it is the custom, as you know, that the sons of wealthy fathers live with their parents in expectation of inheriting the estate. Arkad did not approve of this custom. Therefore, when Nomasir became of age, he sent for the young man and addressed him:

"'My son, it is my desire that you succeed to my estate. You must, however, first prove that you are capable of wisely handling it. Therefore, I wish that you go out into the world and show your ability both to acquire gold and to make yourself respected among others.

"'To start you well, I will give you two things of which I, myself, was denied when I started as a poor youth to build up a fortune.

"'First, I give you this bag of gold. If you use it wisely, it will be the basis of your future success.

"'Second, I give you this clay tablet upon which is carved the five laws of gold. If you interpret them in your own acts, they shall bring you competence and security.

"'Ten years from this day come back to the house of your father and give account of yourself. If you prove worthy, I will then make you the heir to my estate. Otherwise, I will give it to the priests that they may barter for my soul the land consideration of the gods.'

"So Nomasir went forth to make his own way, taking his bag of gold, the clay tablet carefully wrapped in silken cloth, his slave, and the horses upon which they rode.

"The ten years passed, and Nomasir, as he had agreed, returned to the house of his father, who provided a great feast in his honor, to which he invited many friends and relatives. After the feast was over, the father and mother mounted their throne-like seats at one side of the great hall, and Nomasir stood before them to give an account of himself as he had promised.

It was evening. The room was hazy with smoke from the wicks of the oil lamps that dimly lighted it. Slaves in white woven jackets and tunics fanned the humid air rhythmically with long-stemmed palm leaves. A stately dignity colored the scene. The wife of Nomasir and his two young sons, with friends and other members of the family, sat upon rugs behind him, eager listeners.

"'My father,' he began deferentially, I bow before your wisdom. Ten years ago when I stood at the gates of manhood, you bade me go forth and become a man among men instead of remaining a vassal to your fortune.

"'You gave me liberally of your gold. You gave me liberally of your wisdom. Of the gold, alas! I must admit of a disastrous handling. It fled, indeed, from my inexperienced hands even as a wild hare flees at the first opportunity from the youth who captures it.'

"The father smiled indulgently. 'Continue, my son; your tale interests me in all its details.'

"'I decided to go to Nineveh, as it was a growing city, believing that I might find there opportunities. I joined a caravan and among its members made numerous friends. Two well-spoken men who had a most beautiful white horse as fleet as the wind were among these.

"'As we journeyed, they told me in confidence that in Nineveh was a wealthy man who owned a horse so swift that it had never been beaten. Its owner believed that no horse living could run with greater speed. Therefore, would he wager any sum however large that his horse could out-speed any horse in all Babylonia. Compared to their horse, so my friends said, it was but a lumbering ass that could be beaten with ease.

"'They offered, as a great favor, to permit me to join them in a wager. I was quite carried away with the plan.

"'Our horse was badly beaten, and I lost much of my gold.' The father laughed. 'Later, I discovered that this was a deceitful plan of these men and they constantly journeyed with caravans seeking victims. You see, the man in Nineveh was their partner and shared with them the bets he won. This shrewd deceit taught me my first lesson in looking out for myself.

"'I was soon to learn another, equally bitter. In the caravan was another young man with whom I became quite friendly. He was the son of wealthy parents and, like myself, journeying to Nineveh to find a suitable location. Not long after our arrival, he told me that a merchant had died and his shop with its rich merchandise and patronage could be secured at a paltry price. Saying that we would be equal partners but first he must return to Babylon to secure his gold, he prevailed upon me to purchase the stock with my gold, agreeing that his would be used later to carry on our venture.

"'He long delayed the trip to Babylon, proving in the meantime to be an unwise buyer and a foolish spender. I finally put him out, but not before the business had deteriorated to where we had only unsalable goods and no gold to buy other goods. I sacrificed what was left to an Israelite for a pitiful sum.

"'Soon there followed, I tell you, my father, bitter days. I sought employment and found it not, for I was without trade or training that would enable me to earn. I sold my horses. I sold my slave. I sold my extra robes that I might have food and a place to sleep, but each day grim want crouched closer.

"'But in those bitter days, I remembered your confidence in me, my father. You had sent me forth to become a man, and this I was determined to accomplish.' The mother buried her face and wept softly. "'At this time, I bethought me of the table you had given to me upon which you had carved the five laws of gold. Thereupon, I read most carefully your words of wisdom, and I realized that had I but sought wisdom first, my gold would not have been lost to me.

I learned by heart each law and determined that, when once more the goddess of good fortune smiled upon me, I would be guided by the wisdom of age and not by the inexperience of youth.

"'For the benefit of you who are seated here this night, I will read the wisdom of my father as engraved upon the clay tablet which he gave me ten years ago:

The Five Laws of Gold

I. Gold comes gladly and in increasing quantity to any who will put by not less than one-tenth of their earnings to create an estate for their future and that of their family.

II. Gold labors diligently and contentedly for the wise owner who finds for it profitable employment, multiplying even as the flocks of the field.

III. Gold clings to the protection of the cautious owner who invests it under the advice of those wise in its handling.

IV. Gold slips away from those who invest it in businesses or purposes with which they are not familiar or which are not approved by those skilled in its keep.

V. Gold flees those who would force it to impossible earnings or who follow the alluring advice of tricksters and schemers or who trust it to their own inexperience and romantic desires in investment.

"'These are the five laws of gold as written by my father. I proclaim them as of greater value than gold itself, as I will show by the continuance of my tale.'

"He again faced his father. 'I have told you of the depth of poverty and despair to which my inexperience brought me.

"'However, there is no chain of disasters that will not come to an end. Mine came when I secured employment managing a crew of slaves working upon the new outer wall of the city. "

'Profiting from my knowledge of the first law of gold, I saved a copper from my first earnings, adding to it at every opportunity until I had a piece of silver. It was a slow procedure, for one must live. I spent grudgingly, I admit, because I was determined to earn back before the ten years were over as much gold as you, my father, had given me.

"'One day the slave master, with whom I had become quite friendly, said to me, "You are a thrifty youth who spends not wantonly what he earns. Have you gold put by that is not earning?"

"'Yes,' I replied. 'It is my greatest desire to accumulate gold to replace that which my father gave to me and which I have lost.'

"''Tis a worthy ambition, I will grant, and do you know that the gold which you have saved can work for you and earn much more gold?"

"'Alas! my experience has been bitter, for my father's gold has fled from me, and I am in much fear lest my own do the same.'

"'If you have confidence in me, I will give you a lesson in the profitable handling of gold," he replied. "Within a year the outer wall will be complete and ready for the great gates of bronze that will be built at each entrance to protect the city from the king's enemies. In all Nineveh there is not enough metal to make these gates, and the king has not thought to provide it. Here is my plan: A group of us will pool our gold and send a caravan to the mines of copper and tin, which are distant, and bring to Nineveh the metal for the gates. When the king says, 'Make the great gates,' we alone can supply the metal, and a rich price he will pay. If the king will not buy from us, we will yet have the metal which can be sold for a fair price."

"'In his offer I recognized an opportunity to abide by the third law and invest my savings under the guidance of the wise. Nor was

I disappointed. Our pool was a success, and my small store of gold was greatly increased by the transaction.

"In due time, I was accepted as a member of this same group in other ventures. They were wise in the profitable handling of gold. They talked over each plan presented with great care before entering upon it. They would take no chance on losing their principal or tying it up in unprofitable investments from which their gold could not be recovered. Such foolish things as the horse race and the partnership into which I had entered with my inexperience would have had scant consideration with them. They would have immediately pointed out their weaknesses.

"'Through my association with this group, I learned to safely invest gold to bring profitable returns. As the years went on, my treasure increased more and more rapidly. I not only made back as much as I had lost but much more.

"'Through my misfortunes, my trials, and my success, I have tested time and again the wisdom of the five laws of gold, my father, and have proven them true in every test. To those who are without knowledge of the five laws, gold comes not often, and goes away quickly. But to those who abide by the five laws, gold comes and works as their dutiful slave.'

"Nomasir ceased speaking and motioned to a slave in the back of the room. The slave brought forward, one at a time, three heavy leather bags. One of these Nomasir took and placed upon the floor before his father addressing him again:

"'You gave to me a bag of gold, Babylon gold. Behold, in its place I return to you a bag of Nineveh gold of equal weight—an equal exchange, as all will agree.

"'You gave to me a clay tablet inscribed with wisdom. Behold, in its stead, I return two bags of gold.' So saying, he took from the slave the other two bags and, likewise, placed them upon the floor before his father.

"'This I do to prove to you, my father, of how much greater value I consider your wisdom than your gold. Yet who can measure, in bags of gold, the value of wisdom? Without wisdom, gold is quickly lost by those who have it, but with wisdom, gold can be secured by those who have it not, as these three bags of gold prove.

"'It does, indeed, give me the deepest satisfaction, my father, to stand before you and say that, because of your wisdom, I have been able to become rich and respected.'

"The father placed his hand fondly upon the head of Nomasir. 'You have learned well your lessons, and I am, indeed, fortunate to have a son to whom I may entrust my wealth.'

"Kalabab ceased his tale and looked critically at his listeners.

"What means this to you, this tale of Nomasir?" he continued.

"Who among you can go to your father or to the father of your wife and give an account of wise handling of his earnings?

"What would these venerable men think were you to say: 'I have traveled much and learned much and labored much and earned much, yet alas, of gold I have little. Some I spent wisely, some I spent foolishly, and much I lost in unwise ways.'

"Do you still think it but an inconsistency of fate that some have much gold and others have naught? Then you err.

"We have much gold when we know the five laws of gold and abide thereby.

"Because I learned these five laws in my youth and abided by them, I have become a wealthy merchant. Not by some strange magic did I accumulate my wealth.

"Wealth that comes quickly goes the same way.

"Wealth that stays to give enjoyment and satisfaction to its owner comes gradually, because it is a child born of knowledge and persistent purpose.

"To earn wealth is but a slight burden upon those who are thoughtful. Bearing the burden consistently from year to year accomplishes the final purpose.

"The five laws of gold offer you a rich reward for their observance.

"Each of these five laws is rich with meaning, and lest you overlook this in the briefness of my tale, I will now repeat them. I know each one by heart, because in my youth I could see their value and would not be content until I knew them word for word.

The First Law of Gold

Gold comes gladly and in increasing quantity to any who will put by not less than one-tenth of their earnings to create an estate for their future and that of their family.

"Any who will put by one-tenth of their earnings consistently and invest it wisely will surely create a valuable estate that will provide an income for the future and further guarantee safety for their family in case the gods call them to the world of darkness. This law says that gold comes always to such. I can truly certify this in my own life. The more gold I accumulate, the more readily it comes to me, and in increased quantities. The gold which I save earns more, even as yours will, and its earnings earn more, and this is the working out of the first law."

The Second Law of Gold

Gold labors diligently and contentedly for the wise owner who finds for it profitable employment, multiplying even as the flocks of the field.

"Gold, indeed, is a willing worker. It is ever eager to multiply when opportunity presents itself. To all who have a store of gold set by, opportunity comes for its most profitable use. As the years pass, it multiplies itself in surprising fashion."

The Third Law of Gold

Gold clings to the protection of the cautious owner who invests it under the advice of those wise in its handling.

"Gold, indeed, clings to the cautious owner, even as it flees the careless owner. People who seek the advice of those wise in handling gold soon learn not to jeopardize their treasure but to preserve it in safety and to enjoy in contentment its consistent increase."

The Fourth Law of Gold

Gold slips away from those who invest it in businesses or purposes with which they are not familiar or which are not approved by those skilled in its keep.

"To those who have gold yet are not skilled in its handling, many uses for it appear most profitable. Too often these are fraught with danger of loss, and if properly analyzed by the wise, show small possibility of profit. Therefore, the inexperienced owners of gold who trust to their own judgment and invest it in business or purposes with which they are not familiar too often find their judgment imperfect, and they pay with their treasure for their inexperience. Wise, indeed are people who invest their treasures under the advice of those skilled In the ways of gold."

The Fifth Law of Gold

Gold flees those who would force it to impossible earnings, or who follow the alluring advice of tricksters and schemers, or who trust it to their own inexperience and romantic desires in investment.

"Fanciful propositions that thrill like adventure tales always come to the new owners of gold. These appear to endow their treasure with magic powers that will enable it to make impossible earnings. Yet heed the wise, for they know well the risks that lurk behind every plan to make great wealth suddenly.

"Forget not the wealthy citizens of Nineveh who would take no chance of losing their principal or tying it up in unprofitable investments.

"This ends my tale of the five laws of gold. In telling it to you, I have revealed the secrets of my own success.

"Yet they are not secrets but truths which all must first learn and then follow who wish to step out of the multitude that, like you wild dogs, must worry each day for food to eat.

"Tomorrow, we enter Babylon. Look! See the fire that burns eternal above the Temple of Bel! We are already in sight of the golden city. Tomorrow, each of you shall have gold, the gold you have so well earned by your faithful services.

"Ten years from this night, what can you tell about this gold?

"If there be those among you, who, like Nomasir, will use a portion of their gold to start for themselves an estate and be thenceforth wisely guided by the wisdom of Arkad, ten years from now, 'tis a safe wager, like the son of Arkad, they will be rich and respected.

"Our wise acts accompany us through life to please us and to help us. Just as surely, our unwise acts follow us to plague and torment us. Alas, they cannot be forgotten. In the front rank of the torments that follow us are the memories of the things we should have done, of the opportunities which came to us and we took not.

"Rich are the treasures of Babylon, so rich no one can count their value in pieces of gold. Each year they grow richer and more valuable. Like the treasures of every land, they are a reward, a rich reward awaiting those of purpose who determine to secure their just share.

"In the strength of your own desires is a magic power. Guide this power with your knowledge of the five laws of gold, and you shall share the treasures of Babylon."

The Gold Lender of Babylon

Fifty pieces of gold! Never before had Rodan, the spear-maker of old Babylon, carried so much gold in his leather wallet. Happily down the king's highway from the palace of his most liberal Majesty he strode. Cheerfully the gold clinked as the wallet at his belt swayed with each step—the sweetest music he had ever heard.

Fifty pieces of gold! All his! He could hardly realize his good fortune. What power in those clinking discs! They could purchase anything he wanted, a grand house, land, cattle, camels, horses, chariots, whatever he might desire.

What use should he make of it? This evening as he turned into a side street towards the home of his sister, he could think of nothing he would rather possess than those same glittering, heavy pieces of gold—his to keep.

It was upon an evening some days later that a perplexed Rodan entered the shop of Mathon, the lender of gold and dealer in jewels and rare fabrics. Glancing neither to the right nor the left at the colorful articles artfully displayed, he passed through to the living quarters at the rear. Here he found the genteel Mathon lounging upon a rug partaking of a meal served by a black slave.

"I would counsel with you for I know not what to do." Rodan

stood stolidly, feet apart, hairy breast exposed by the gaping front of his leather jacket.

Mathon's narrow, sallow face smiled a friendly greeting. "What indiscretions have you done that you should seek the lender of gold? Have you been unlucky at the gaming table? Or has some plump dame entangled you? For many years I have known you, yet never have you sought me to aid you in your troubles."

"No, no. Not such as that. I seek no gold. Instead I crave your wise advice."

"Hear! Hear! What this man does say. No one comes to the lender of gold for advice. My ears must play me false."

"They listen true."

"Can this be so? Rodan, the spear-maker, displays more cunning than all the rest, for he comes to Mathon, not for gold but for advice. Many come to me for gold to pay for their follies, but as for advice, they want it not. Yet who is more able to advise than the lender of gold to whom many come in trouble?

"You shall eat with me, Rodan," he continued. You shall be my guest for the evening. Andol" he commanded of the slave, "draw up a rag for my friend, Rodan, the spear-maker, who comes for advice. He shall be my honored guest. Bring him much food and get for him my largest cup. Choose well of the best wine that he may have satisfaction in the drinking.

"Now, tell me what troubles you."

"It is the king's gift."

"The king's gift? The king made you a gift and it gives you trouble? What manner of gift?"

"Because he was much pleased with the design I submitted to him for a new point on the spears of the royal guard, he presented me with fifty pieces of gold, and now I am much perplexed, for I am beseeched each hour the sun travels across the sky by those who would share it with me."

"That is natural. More people want gold than have it, and would wish one who comes by it easily to divide. But can you not say 'No?' Is your will not as strong as your fist?"

"To many I can say no, yet sometimes it would be easier to say yes. Can one refuse to share with one's sister to whom he is deeply devoted?"

"Surely, your own sister would not wish to deprive you of enjoying your reward."

"But it is for the sake of Araman, her husband, whom she wishes to see a rich merchant. She feels that he has never had a chance, and she beseeches me to loan him this gold that he may become a prosperous merchant and repay me from his profits."

"My friend," resumed Mathon, "'tis a worthy subject you bring to discuss. Gold brings to its possessors responsibility and a changed position with their fellows. It brings fear lest they lose it or it be tricked away from them. It brings a feeling of power and ability to do good. Likewise, it brings opportunities whereby their very good intentions may bring them into difficulties.

"Did you ever hear of the farmer of Nineveh who could understand the language of animals? I wot not, for 'tis not the kind of tale folk like to tell over the bronze caster's forge. I will tell it to you, for you should know that to borrowing and lending there is more than the passing of gold from the hands of one to the hands of another.

"This farmer, who could understand what the animals said to each other, lingered in the farm yard each evening just to listen to their words. One evening he heard the ox bemoaning to the ass the hardness of his lot: 'I labor pulling the plow from morning until night. No matter how hot the day, or how tired my legs, or how the bow chafes my neck, still I must work. But you are a creature of leisure. You are trapped with a colorful blanket and do nothing more than carry our master about where he wishes to go. When he goes nowhere you rest and eat the green grass all the day.'

"Now the ass, in spite of his vicious heels, was a goodly fellow and sympathized with the ox. 'My good friend, he replied, 'you do work hard, and I would help ease your lot. Therefore, I will tell you how you may have a day of rest. In the morning when the slave comes to fetch you to the plow, lie upon the ground and bellow that he may say you are sick and cannot work.'

"So the ox took the advice of the ass, and the next morning the slave returned to the farmer and told him the ox was sick and could not pull the plow.

"'Then,' said the farmer, "hitch the ass to the plow„ for the plowing must go on.'

"All that day the ass, who had only intended to help his friend, found himself compelled to do the ox's task. When night came and he was released from the plow, his heart was bitter and his legs were weary, and his neck was sore where the bow had chafed it.

"The farmer lingered in the barnyard to listen.

"The ox began first. 'You are my good friend. Because of your wise advice I have enjoyed a day of rest.'

"'And I,' retorted the ass, 'am like many another simplehearted one who wantss to help friends and ends up doing their tasks. Hereafter you draw your own plow, for I heard the master tell the slave to send for the butcher if you were sick again. I wish he would, for you are a lazy fellow.' Thereafter they spoke to each other no more—this ended their friendship. Can you tell the moral to this tale, Rodan?"

"'Tis a good tale," responded Rodan, "but I see not the moral."

"I thought not that you would. But it is there and simple too. Just this: If you desire to help your friends, do so in a way that will not bring your friends' burdens upon yourself."

"I had not thought of that. It is a wise moral. I wish not to assume the burdens of my sister's husband. But tell me: You lend to many. Do not the borrowers repay?"

Mathon smiled the smile of one whose soul is rich with much experience. "Could a loan be well made if the borrower cannot repay? Must not lenders be wise and judge carefully whether their gold can perform a useful purpose to borrowers and return to the lenders once more? or whether it will be wasted by those unable to use it wisely and leave the lenders without their treasure, and the borrowers with a debt that they cannot repay? I will show to you the tokens in my token chest and let them tell you some of their stories."

Into the room he brought a chest as long as his arm covered with red pigskin and ornamented with bronze designs. He placed it upon the floor and squatted before it, both hands upon the lid.

"From each person to whom I lend, I exact a token for my token chest, to remain there until the loan is repaid. When they repay I give back the token, but if they never repay, it will always remind me of one who was not faithful to my confidence.

"The safest loans, my token box tells me, are to those whose possessions are of more value than the loan they desire. They own lands, or jewels, or camels, or other things which could be sold to repay the loan. Some of the tokens given to me are jewels of more value than the loan. Others are promises that if the loan be not repaid as agreed, they will deliver to me certain property as settlement. On loans like those, I am assured that my gold will be returned with the rental thereon, for the loan is based on property.

"In another class are those who have the capacity to earn. They are such as you, who labor or serve and are paid. They have income, and if they are honest and suffer no misfortune, I know that they also can repay the gold I loan them and the rental to which I am entitled. Such loans are based on human effort.

"Others are those who have neither property nor assured earning capacity. Life is hard, and there will always be some who cannot adjust themselves to it. Alas for the loans I make to them! Even though they be no larger than a pence, my token box may censure me in the years to come unless such loans are guaranteed by good friends of the borrowers who know them to be honorable."

Mathon released the clasp and opened the lid. Rodan leaned forward eagerly.

At the top of the chest a bronze neck-piece lay upon a scarlet cloth. Mathon picked up the piece and patted it affectionately. "This shall always remain in my token chest because the owner has passed on into the great darkness. I treasure it, his token, and I treasure his memory, for he was my good friend. We traded together with much success until out of the east he brought a woman to wed, beautiful, but not like our women. A dazzling creature. He spent his gold lavishly to gratify her desires. He came to me in distress when his gold was gone. I counseled with him. I told him I would help him to once more master his own affairs. He swore by the sign of the Great Bull that he would. But it was not to be. In a quarrel she thrust a knife into the heart he dared her to pierce."

"And she?" questioned Rodan. "Yes, of course, this was hers." He picked up the scarlet cloth. "In bitter remorse she threw herself into the Euphrates. These two loans will never be repaid. The chest tells you, Rodan, that humans in the throes of great emotions are not safe risks for the gold lender.

"Here! Now this is different." He reached for a ring carved of ox bone. "This belongs to a farmer. I buy the rugs from the women of his household. The locusts came, and the family had no food. I helped him, and when the new crop came he repaid me. Later he came again and told of strange goats in a distant land as described by a traveler. They had long hair so fine and soft it would weave into rugs more beautiful than any ever seen in Babylon. He wanted a herd but he had no money. So I lent him gold to make the journey and bring back goats. Now his herd is begun, and next year I shall surprise the lords of Babylon with the most expensive rugs it has been their good fortune to buy. Soon I must return his ring, for he insists on repaying promptly."

"Some borrowers do that?" queried Rodan.

"If they borrow for purposes that bring money back to them, I find it so. But if they borrow because of their indiscretions, I warn you to be cautious if you would ever have your gold back in hand again."

"Tell me about this," requested Rodan, picking up a heavy gold bracelet inset with jewels in rare designs.

"The women do appeal to my good friend," bantered Mathon.

"I am still much younger than you," retorted Rodan.

"I grant that, but this time you suspicion romance where it is not. The owner of this is fat and wrinkled, and she talks so much and says so little she drives me mad. Once she and her family had much money and were good customers, but ill times came upon them. She has a son of whom she would make a merchant. So she came to me and borrowed gold that he might become a partner of a caravan owner who travels with his camels, bartering in one city what he buys in another.

"This man proved a rascal, for he left the poor boy in a distant city without money and without friends, pulling out early while the youth slept. Perhaps when this youth has grown to manhood, he will repay; until then I get no rental for the loan—only much talk. But I do admit the jewels are worthy of the loan."

"Did this lady ask your advice as to the wisdom of the loan?"

"Quite otherwise. She had pictured to herself this son of hers as a wealthy and powerful man of Babylon. To suggest the contrary was to infuriate her. A fair rebuke I had. I knew the risk for this inexperienced boy, but as she offered security I could not refuse her.

"This," continued Mathon, waving a bit of pack rope tied into a knot, "belongs to Nebatur, the camel trader. When he would buy a herd larger than his funds, he brings to me this knot, and I lend to him according to his needs. He is a wise trader. I have confidence in his good judgment and can lend him freely. Many other merchants of Babylon have my confidence because of their honorable behavior. Their tokens come and go frequently in my token box. Good merchants are an asset to our city, and it profits me to aid them to keep trade moving that Babylon be prosperous."

Mathon picked out a beetle carved in turquoise and tossed it contemptuously on the floor. "A bug from Egypt. The lad who owns this does not care whether I ever receive back my gold. When I reproach him he replies, 'How can I repay when ill fate pursues me? You have plenty more.' What can I do? The token is his father's—a worthy man of small means who pledged his land and herd to back his son's enterprises. The youth found success at first and then was over-zealous to gain great wealth. His knowledge was immature, and his enterprises collapsed.

"Youth is ambitious. Youth would take short-cuts to wealth and the desirable things for which it stands. To secure wealth quickly, youth often borrows unwisely.

Youth, never having had experience, cannot realize that hopeless debt is like a deep pit into which one may descend quickly and where one may struggle vainly for many days. It is a pit of sorrow and regrets, where the brightness of the sun is overcast and night is made unhappy by restless sleeping. Yet, I do not discourage borrowing gold. I encourage it. I recommend it if it be for a wise purpose. I myself made my first real success as a merchant with borrowed gold.

"Yet, what should the lender do in such a case? The youth is in despair and accomplishes nothing. He is discouraged. He makes no effort to repay. My heart turns against depriving the father of his land and cattle."

"You tell me much that I am interested to hear," ventured Rodan, "but, I hear no answer to my question. Should I lend my fifty pieces of gold to my sister's husband? They mean much to me."

"Thy sister is a sterling woman whom I much esteem. Should her husband come to me and ask to borrow fifty pieces of gold, I should ask him for what purpose he would use it.

"If he answered that he desired to become a merchant like myself and deal in jewels and rich furnishings, I would say, 'What knowledge have you of the ways of trade? Do you know where you can buy at lowest cost? Do you know where you can sell at a fair price?' Could he say 'Yes' to these questions?"

"No, he could not," Rodan admitted. "He has helped me much in making spears, and he has helped some in the shops."

"Then would I say to him that his purpose is not wise. Merchants must learn their trade. His ambition, though worthy, is not practical, and I would not lend him any gold.

"But, supposing he could say: 'Yes, I have helped merchants much. I know how to travel to Smyrna and to buy at low cost the rugs the artisans weave. I also know many of the rich people of Babylon to whom I can sell these at a large profit.' Then I would say: 'Your purpose is wise and your ambition honorable. I shall be glad to lend you the fifty pieces of gold if you can give me security that they will be returned.' But would he say, 'I have no security other than that I am an honored man and will pay you well for the loan.' Then would I reply, 'I treasure much each piece of gold. Were the robbers to take it from you as you journeyed to Smyrna or take the rugs from you as you returned, then you would have no means of repaying me, and my gold would be gone.'

"Gold, you see, Rodan, is the merchandise of the lender of money. It is easy to lend. If it is lent unwisely, then it is difficult to get back. The wise lender wishes not the risk of the undertaking but the guarantee of safe repayment.

"'Tis well," he continued, "to assist those that are in trouble. 'Tis well to help those upon whom fate has laid a heavy hand. 'Tis well to help those who are starting that they may progress and become valuable citizens. But help must be given wisely, lest, like the farmer's ass, in our desire to help we but take upon ourselves the burden that belongs to another.

"Again I wandered from your question, Rodan, but hear my answer: Keep your fifty pieces of gold. What your labor earns for you and what is given you for reward is your own, and no one can put an obligation upon you to part with it unless it be your wish. If you would lend it so that it may earn you more gold, then lend with caution and in many places. I like not idle gold; even less I like too much of risk.

"How many years have you labored as a spear-maker?"

"Fully three."

"How much besides the king's gift have you saved?"

"Three gold pieces."

"Each year that you have labored you have denied yourself good things to save from yours earnings one piece of gold?"

"'Tis as you say."

"Then you mightest save in fifty years of labor fifty pieces of gold by your self-denial?"

"A lifetime of labor it would be."

"Do you think your sister would wish to jeopardize the savings of fifty years of labor over the bronze melting pot that her husband might experiment on being a merchant?"

"Not if I spoke in your words."

"Then go to her and say: 'Three years I have labored each day except fast days, from morning until night, and I have denied myself many things that my heart craved. For each year of labor and self-denial, I have to show one piece of gold. You are my favored sister, and I wish that your husband may engage in business in which he will prosper greatly. If he will submit to me a plan that seems wise and possible to my friend, Mathon, then I will gladly lend to him my savings of an entire year that he may have an opportunity to prove that he can succeed.' Do that, I say, and if he has within him the soul to succeed, he can prove it. If he fails, he will not owe you more than he can hope someday to repay.

"I am a gold lender because I own more gold than I can use in my own trade. I desire my surplus gold to labor for others and thereby earn more gold. I do not wish to risk losing my gold, for I have labored much and denied myself much to secure it. Therefore, I will no longer lend any of it where I am not confident that it is safe and will be returned to me. Neither will I lend it where I am not convinced that its earnings will be promptly paid to me.

"I have told you, Rodan, a few of the secrets of my token chest. From them you may understand people's weakness and their eagerness to borrow that which they have no certain means to repay. From this you can see how often their high hopes of the great earnings they could make, if they but had gold, are but false hopes they have not the ability or training to fulfill.

"You, Rodan, now have gold which you should put to earning more gold for you. You are about to become even as I, a gold lender. If you safely preserve your treasure, it will produce liberal earnings for you and be a rich source of pleasure and profit during all your days. But if you let it escape from you, it will be a source of constant sorrow and regret as long as your memory lasts.

"What desire you most of this gold in your wallet?"

"To keep it safe."

"Wisely spoken," replied Mathon approvingly. "Your first desire is for safety. Do you think that in the custody of your sister's husband it would be truly safe from possible loss?"

"I fear not, for he is not wise in guarding gold."

"Then be not swayed by foolish sentiments of obligation to trust your treasure to any person. If you would help your family or your friends, find other ways than risking the loss of your treasure. Forget not that gold slips away in unexpected ways from those unskilled in guarding it. As well waste your treasure in extravagance as let others lose it for you.

"What next after safety do you desire from this treasure of yours?"

"That it earn more gold."

"Again you speak with wisdom. It should be made to earn and grow larger. Gold wisely lent may even double itself with its earnings before one like you grows old. If you risk losing it, you risk losing all that it would earn as well.

"Therefore, be not swayed by the fantastic plans of impractical people who think they see ways to force your gold to make earnings unusually large. Such plans are the creations of dreamers unskilled in the safe and dependable laws of trade. Be conservative in what you expect it to earn that you may keep and enjoy your treasure. To hire it out with a promise of usurious returns is to invite loss.

"Seek to associate yourself with people and enterprises whose success is established, that your treasure may earn liberally under their skillful use and be guarded safely by their wisdom and experience.

"Thus may you avoid the misfortunes that follow most of those to whom the gods see fit to entrust gold."

When Rodan would thank him for his wise advice, he would not listen, saying, "The king's gift shall teach you much wisdom. If would keep your fifty pieces of gold, you must be discreet indeed. Many uses will tempt you. Much advice will be spoken to you. Numerous opportunities to make large profits will be offered you. The stories from my token box should warn you, before you let any piece of gold leave your pouch, to be sure that you have a safe way to pull it back again. Should my further advice appeal to you, return again. It is gladly given.

"'E're you go, read this which I have carved beneath the lid of my token box. It applies equally to the borrower and the lender:

Better a little caution than a great regret.

The Walls of Babylon

Old Banzar, grim warrior of another day, stood guard at the passageway leading to the top of the ancient walls of Babylon. Up above, valiant defenders were battling to hold the walls. Upon them depended the future existence of this great city with its hundreds of thousands of citizens.

Over the walls came the roar of the attacking armies, the yelling of many soldiers, the trampling of thousands of horses, the deafening boom of the battering rams pounding the bronzed gates.

In the street behind the gate lounged the spear-guards, waiting to defend the entrance should the gates give way. They were but few for the task. The main armies of Babylon were with their king, far away in the east on the great expedition against the Elamites. No attack upon the city having been anticipated during their absence, the defending forces were small. Unexpectedly, from the north, bore down the mighty armies of the Assyrians. And now the walls must hold or Babylon was doomed.

About Banzar were great crowds of citizens, white-faced and terrified, eagerly seeking news of the battle. With hushed awe they viewed the stream of wounded and dead being carried or led out of the passageway.

Here was the crucial point of attack. After three days of circling about the city, the enemy had suddenly thrown their great strength against this section and this gate.

The defenders from the top of the wall fought off the climbing platforms and the scaling ladders of the attackers with arrows, burning oil, and, if any reached the top, spears. Against the defenders, thousands of the enemy's archers poured a deadly barrage of arrows.

Old Banzar had the vantage point for news. He was closest to the conflict and first to hear of each fresh repulse of the frenzied attackers.

An elderly merchant crowded close to him, his palsied hands quivering. "Tell me! Tell me!" he pleaded. "They cannot get in. My sons are with the good king. There is no one to protect my old wife. My goods, they will steal all. My food, they will leave nothing. We are old, too old to defend ourselves—too old to be slaves. We shall starve. We shall die. Tell me they cannot get in."

"Calm yourself, good merchant," the guard responded. "The walls of Babylon are strong. Go back to the bazaar and tell your wife that the walls will protect you and all of your possessions as safely as they protect the rich treasures of the king. Keep close to the walls, lest the arrows flying over strike you!"

A woman with a babe in arms took the old man's place as he withdrew. "Sergeant, what news from the top? Tell me truly that I may reassure my poor husband. He lies with fever from his terrible wounds, yet insists upon his armor and his spear to protect me, who am with child. Terrible, he says will be the vengeful lust of our enemies should they break in."

"Be of good heart, you mother that is, and is again to be. The walls of Babylon will protect you and your babes. They are high and strong. Do you not hear the yells of our valiant defenders as they empty the caldrons of burning oil upon the ladder scalers?"

"Yes, that I hear, and also the roar of the battering rams that hammer at our gates."

"Back to your husband. Tell him the gates are strong and withstand the rams. Also that the scalers climb the walls but to receive the waiting spear thrust. Watch your way and hasten behind the buildings."

Banzar stepped aside to clear the passage for heavily armed reinforcements. As, with clanking bronze shields and heavy tread they tramped by, a small girl plucked at his girdle.

"Tell me please, soldier, are we safe?" she pleaded. I hear the awful noises. I see the warriors all bleeding. I am so frightened. What will become of our family, of my mother, little brother, and the baby?"

The grim old campaigner blinked his eyes and thrust forward his chin as he beheld the child.

"Be not afraid, little one," he reassured her. "The walls of Babylon will protect you and mother and little brother and the baby. It was for the safety of such as you that the good Queen Semiramis built them more than a hundred years ago. Never have they been broken through. Go back and tell your mother and little brother and the baby that the walls of Babylon will protect them and they need have no fear."

Day after day old Banzar stood at his post and watched the reinforcements file up the passageway, there to stay and fight until wounded or dead they came down once more. Around him unceasingly crowded the throngs of frightened citizens eagerly seeking to learn if the walls would hold. To all he gave his answer with the fine dignity of an old soldier, "The walls of Babylon will protect you."

For three weeks and five days the attack waged with scarcely ceasing violence. Harder and grimmer set the jaw of Banzar as the passage behind, wet with the blood of the many wounded, was churned into mud by the never ceasing streams of soldiers passing up and staggering down. Each day the slaughtered attackers piled up in heaps before the wall. Each night they were carried back and buried by their comrades. Upon the fifth night of the fourth week, the clamor without diminished. The first streaks of daylight, illuminating the plains, disclosed great clouds of dust raised by the retreating armies.

A mighty shout went up from the defenders. There was no mistaking its meaning. It was repeated by the waiting troops behind the walls. It was echoed by the citizens upon the streets. It swept over the city with the violence of a storm.

People rushed from the houses. The streets were jammed with a throbbing mob. The pent-up fear of weeks found an outlet in the wild chorus of joy. From the top of the high tower of the Temple of Bel burst forth the flames of victory. Skyward floated the column of blue smoke to carry the message far and wide.

The walls of Babylon had once again repulsed a mighty foe determined to loot her rich treasures and to ravish and enslave her citizens.

Babylon endured century after century because it was fully protected. It could not afford to be otherwise.

The walls of Babylon were an outstanding example of our need and desire for protection. This desire is inherent in the human race. It is just as strong today as it ever was, but we have developed broader and better plans to accomplish the same purpose.

In this day, behind the impregnable walls of insurance, savings accounts, and dependable investments, we can guard ourselves against the unexpected tragedies that may enter any door and seat themselves before any fireside.

We cannot afford to be without adequate protection.

The Camel Trader of Babylon

The hungrier one becomes, the clearer one's mind works—also the more sensitive one becomes to the odors of food.

Tarkad, the son of Azure, certainly thought so. For two whole days he had tasted no food except two small figs purloined from over the wall of a garden. Not another could he grab before the angry woman rushed forth and chased him down the street. Her shrill cries were still ringing in his ears as he walked through the marketplace. They helped him restrain his restless fingers from snatching the tempting fruits from the baskets of the merchants.

Never before had he realized how much food was brought to the markets of Babylon and how good it smelled. Leaving the market, he walked across to the inn and paced back and forth in front of the eating house. Perhaps here he might meet someone he knew, someone from whom he could borrow a copper that would gain him a smile from the unfriendly keeper of the inn and, with it, a liberal helping. Without the copper he knew all too well how unwelcome he would be.

In his abstraction he unexpectedly found himself face to face with the one man he wished most to avoid, the tall bony figure of Dabasir, the camel trader. Of all the friends and others from whom he had borrowed small sums, Dabasir made him feel the most uncomfortable because of his failure to keep his promises to repay promptly.

Dabasir's face lighted up at the sight of him. "Ha! 'Tis Tarkad, just the one I have been seeking that he might repay the two pieces of copper I lent him a moon ago; also the piece of silver I lent him before that. We are well met. I can make good use of the coins this very day. What say, boy? What say?"

Tarkad stuttered and his face flushed. He had naught in his empty stomach to nerve him to argue with the outspoken Dabasir. "I am sorry, very sorry," he mumbled weakly, "but this day I have neither the copper nor the silver with which I could repay."

"Then get it," Dabasir insisted. "Surely you can get hold of a few coppers and a piece of silver to repay the generosity of an old friend of your father who aided you when you were in need?"

"'Tis because ill fortune pursues me that I cannot pay."

"Ill fortune! Would you blame the gods for your own weakness. Ill fortune pursues all who think more of borrowing than of repaying. Come with me, boy, while I eat. I am hungry and I would tell you a tale."

Tarkad flinched from the brutal frankness of Dabasir, but here at least was an invitation to enter the coveted doorway of the eating house.

Dabasir pushed him to a far corner of the room where they seated themselves upon small rugs.

When Kauskor, the proprietor, appeared smiling, Dabasir addressed him with his usual freedom, "Fat lizard of the desert, bring to me a leg of the goat, brown with much juice, and bread and all of the vegetables, for I am hungry and want much food. Do not forget my friend here. Bring to him a jug of water. Have it cooled, for the day is hot."

Tarkad's heart sank. Must he sit here and drink water while he watched this man devour an entire goat leg? He said nothing. He thought of nothing he could say.

Dabasir, however, knew no such thing as silence. Smiling and waving his hand good-naturedly to the other customers, all of whom knew him, he continued.

"I heard from a traveler just returned from Urfa of a certain rich man who has a piece of stone cut so thin that one can look through it. He put it in the window of his house to keep out the rains. It is yellow, so this traveler relates, and he was permitted to look through it, and all the outside world looked strange and not like it really is. What say you to that, Tarkad? Do you think all the world could look a different color from what it is?"

"I dare say," responded the youth, much more interested in the fat leg of goat placed before Dabasir.

"Well, I know it to be true, for I myself have seen the world all of a different color from what it really is, and the tale I am about to tell relates how I came to see it in its right color once more."

"Dabasir will tell a tale," whispered a neighboring diner to his neighbor, and dragged his rug close. Other diners brought their food and crowded in a semi-circle. They crunched noisily in the ears of Tarkad and brushed him with their meaty bones. He alone was without food. Dabasir did not offer to share with him nor even motion him to a small corner of the hard bread that was broken off and had fallen from the platter to the floor.

"The tale that I am about to tell," began Dabasir, pausing to bite a goodly chunk from the goat leg, "relates to my early life and how I came to be a camel trader. Did anyone know that I once was a slave in Syria?"

A murmur of surprise ran through the audience to which Dabasir listened with satisfaction.

"When I was a young man," continued Dabasir after another

vicious onslaught on the goat leg, "I learned the trade of my father, the making of saddles. I worked with him in his shop and took to myself a wife.

Being young and not greatly skilled, I could earn but little, just enough to support my excellent wife in a modest way. I craved good things which I could not afford. Soon I found that the shopkeepers would trust me to pay later even though I could not pay at the time.

"Being young and without experience, I did not know that those who spend more than they earn are sowing the winds of needless self-indulgence from which they are sure to reap the whirlwinds of trouble and humiliation. So I indulged my whims for fine raiment and bought luxuries for my good wife and our home, beyond our means.

"I paid as I could, and for a while all went well. But in time I discovered I could not use my earnings both to live upon and to pay my debts. Creditors began to pursue me to pay for my extravagant purchases, and my life became miserable. I borrowed from my friends but could not repay them either. Things went from bad to worse. My wife returned to her father, and I decided to leave Babylon and seek another city where I might have better chances.

"For two years I had a restless and unsuccessful life working for caravan traders. From this I fell in with a set of likeable robbers who scoured the desert for unarmed caravans. Such deeds were unworthy of the son of my father, but I was seeing the world through a colored stone and did not realize to what degradation I had fallen.

"We met with success on our first trip, capturing a rich haul of gold and silks and valuable merchandise. This loot we took to Ginir and squandered.

"The second time we were not so fortunate. Just after we had made our capture, we were attacked by the warriors of a native chief to whom the caravans paid for protection. Our two leaders were killed, and the rest of us were taken to Damascus, where we were stripped of our clothing and sold as slaves.

"I was purchased for two pieces of silver by a Syrian desert chief. With my hair shorn and but a loincloth to wear, I was not so different from the other slaves. Being a reckless youth, I thought it merely an adventure until my master took me before his four wives and told them they could have me for a eunuch.

Then, indeed, did I realize the hopelessness of my situation. These people of the desert were fierce and warlike. I was subject to their will without weapons or means of escape.

"Fearful I stood as those four women looked me over. I wondered if I could expect pity from them. Sira, the first wife, was older than the others. Her face was impassive as she looked upon me. I turned from her with little consolation. The next was a contemptuous beauty who gazed at me as indifferently as if I had been a worm of the earth. The two younger ones tittered as though it were all an exciting joke.

"It seemed an age that I stood waiting sentence. Each woman appeared willing for the others to decide. Finally Sira spoke up in a cold voice.

"'Of eunuchs we have plenty, but of camel tenders we have few, and they are a worthless lot. Even this day I would visit my mother who is sick with the fever, and there is no slave I would trust to lead my camel. Ask this slave if he can lead a camel.'

"My master thereupon questioned me, 'What know you of camels?'

"Striving to conceal my eagerness, I replied, I can make them kneel, I can load them, I can lead them on long trips without tiring. If need be, I can repair their trappings."

"'The slave speaks forward enough,' observed my master. 'If you so desire, Sira, take this man for your camel tender.'

"So I was turned over to Sira, and that day I led her camel upon a long journey to her sick mother. I took the occasion to thank her for her intercession and also to tell her that I was not a slave by birth but the son of a freeman, an honorable saddlemaker of Babylon. I also told her much of my story. Her comments were disconcerting to me, and I pondered much afterward on what she said.

"'How can you call yourself a free man when your weakness has brought you to this? If you have in yourself the soul of a slave, will you not become one no matter what your birth, even as water seeks its level? If you have within yourself the soul of one who is free, will you not become respected and honored in your own city in spite of your misfortune?'

"For more than a year I was a slave and lived with the slaves, but I could not become as one of them. One day Sira asked me, 'In the eventime when the other slaves can mingle and enjoy the society of each other, why do you sit in your tent alone?'

"To which I responded, 'I am pondering what you have said to me. I wonder if I have the soul of a slave. I cannot join them, so I must sit apart.'

"'I, too, must sit apart,' she confided. 'My dowry was large, and my lord married me because of it. Yet he does not desire me, although I long to be desired. Because of this, and because I am barren and have neither son nor daughter, I must sit apart. If I were a man, I would rather die than be such a slave, but the conventions of our tribe make slaves of women.'

"'What think you of me by this time?' I asked her suddenly, 'Have I the soul of one who is free, or have I the soul of a slave?'

"'Have you a desire to repay the just debts you owe in Babylon?' she parried.

"'Yes, I have the desire, but I see no way.'

"'If you contentedly let the years slip by and make no effort to repay, then you have but the contemptible soul of a slave. Otherwise, you do not repect yourself, and you cannot respect yourself if you do not repay honest debts.'

"'But what can I do who am a slave in Syria?'

"'Stay a slave in Syria, you weakling.'

"'I am not a weakling,' I denied hotly.

"'Then prove it.'

"'How?'

"'Does not your great king fight his enemies in every way he can and with every force he has? Your debts are your enemies. They ran you out of Babylon. You left them alone and they grew too strong for you. If you had truly fought them, you could have conquered them and been one honored among the townspeople. But you had not the soul to fight them, and your pride has gone down until you are a slave in Syria.'

"Much I thought over her unkind accusations, and many defensive phrases I worded to prove myself not a slave at heart, but I was not to have the chance to use them. Three days later the maid of Sira took me to her mistress.

"'My mother is again very sick,' she said. 'Saddle the two best camels in my husband's herd. Tie on water skins and saddlebags for a long journey. The maid will give you food at the kitchen tent.' I packed the camels, wondering much at the quantity of provisions the maid provided, for the mother dwelt less than a day's journey away. The maid rode the rear camel which followed, and I led the camel of my mistress. When we reached her mother's house it was just dark. Sira dismissed the maid and said to me:

"'Dabasir, have you the soul of one who is free, or the soul of a slave?'

"'The soul of one who is free,' I insisted.

"'Now is your chance to prove it. Your master has imbibed deeply, and his chiefs are in a stupor. Take these camels and make your escape. Here in this bag is raiment of your master's to disguise you. I will say you stole the camels and ran away while I visited my sick mother.'

"'You have the soul of a queen,' I told her. 'Much do I wish that I might lead you to happiness.'

"'Happiness,' she responded, 'awaits not the runaway wife who seeks it in far lands among strange people. Go your own way, and may the gods of the desert protect you, for the way is far and barren of food or water.'

"I needed no further urging but thanked her warmly and was away into the night. I knew not this strange country and had only a dim idea of the direction in which lay Babylon, but I struck out bravely across the desert toward the hills. One camel I rode and the other I led. All that night I traveled and all the next day, urged on by the knowledge of the terrible fate that was meted out to slaves who stole their master's property and tried to escape.

"Late that afternoon, I reached a rough country as uninhabitable as the desert. The sharp rocks bruised the feet of my faithful camels, and soon they were picking their way slowly and painfully along. I met neither man nor beast and could well understand why they shunned this inhospitable land.

"It was such a journey from then on as few live to tell of. Day after day we plodded along. Food and water gave out. The heat of the sun was merciless. At the end of the ninth day, I slid from the back of my mount with the feeling that I was too weak to ever remount, and that I would surely die, lost in this abandoned country.

"I stretched out upon the ground and slept, not waking until the first gleam of daylight.

"I sat up and looked about me. There was a coolness in the morning air. My camels lay dejected not far away. About me was a vast waste of broken country covered with rock and sand and thorny things, no sign of water, naught to eat for man or camel.

"Could it be that in this peaceful quiet I faced my end? My mind was clearer than it had ever been before. My body now seemed of little importance. My parched and bleeding lips, my dry and swollen tongue, my empty stomach, all had lost their supreme agonies of the day before.

"I looked across into the uninviting distance and once again came to me the question, 'Have I the soul of a slave or the soul of a free man?' Then with clearness I realized that if I had the soul of a slave, I should give up, lie down in the desert, and die, a fitting end for a runaway slave.

"But if I had the soul of one who is free, what then? Surely I would force my way back to Babylon, repay those who had trusted me, bring happiness to my wife who truly loved me, and bring peace and contentment to my parents.

"'Your debts are yours enemies who have run you out of Babylon,' Sira had said. Yes it was so. Why had I refused to stand my ground? Why had I permitted my wife to go back to her father?

"Then a strange thing happened. All the world seemed to be of a different color, as though I had been looking at it through a colored stone which had suddenly been removed. At last I saw the true values in life.

"Die in the desert! Not I! With a new vision, I saw the things that I must do. First I would go back to Babylon and face every person to whom I owed an unpaid debt. I should tell them that after years of wandering and misfortune, I had come back to pay my debts as fast as the gods would permit. Next I would make a home for my wife and become a citizen of whom my parents would be proud.

"My debts were my enemies, but those I owed were my friends, for they had trusted me and believed in me.

"I staggered weakly to my feet. What mattered hunger? What mattered thirst? They were but incidents on the road to Babylon. Within me surged the soul of one going back to conquer his enemies and reward his friends. I thrilled with the great resolve.

"The glazed eyes of my camels brightened at the new note in my husky voice. With great effort, after many attempts, they gained their feet. With pitiful perseverance, they pushed on toward the north, where something within me said we would find Babylon.

"We found water. We passed into a more fertile country with grass and fruit. We found the trail to Babylon because the soul of one who is free looks at life as a series of problems to be solved and solves them, while the soul of a slave whines, 'What can I do who am but a slave?'

"How about you, Tarkad? Does your empty stomach make your head exceedingly clear? Are you ready to take the road that leads back to self-respect? Can you see the world in its true color? Have you the desire to pay your honest debts, however many they may be, and once again be respected in Babylon?"

Moisture came to the eyes of the youth. He rose eagerly to his knees. "You have shown me a vision; already I feel the soul of freedom surge within me."

"But how fared you upon your return?" questioned an interested listener.

"Where the determination is, the way can be found" Dabasir replied.

"I now had the determination, so I set out to find a way. First I visited every person to whom I was indebted and begged their indulgence until I could earn that with which to repay. Most of them met me gladly. Several reviled me, but others offered to help me; one indeed gave me the very help I needed. It was Mathon, the gold lender. Learning that I had been a camel tender in Syria, he sent me to old Nebatur, the camel trader, just commissioned by our good king to purchase many herds of sound camels for the great expedition. With him, my knowledge of camels I put to good use. Gradually I was able to repay every copper and every piece of silver. Then at last I could hold up my head and feel that I was an honorable person, free at last."

Again Dabasir turned to his food. "Kauskor, you snail," he called loudly to be heard in the kitchen, "the food is cold. Bring me more meat fresh from the roasting. Bring also a large portion for Tarkad, the son of my old friend, who is hungry and shall eat with me."

So ended the tale of Dabasir the camel trader of old Babylon. He found his own soul when he realized a great truth, a truth that had been known and used by the wise long before his time.

It has led people of all ages out of difficulties and into success, and it will continue to do so for those who have the wisdom to understand its magic power. It is for anyone to use who reads these lines.

Where the determination is, the way can be found.

The Clay Tablets
from Babylon

Tablet No. I

Now, when the moon becomes full, I, Dabasir, who have but recently returned from slavery in Syria, with the determination to pay my many just debts and become worthy of respect in my native city of Babylon, do here engrave upon the clay a permanent record of my affairs to guide and assist me in carrying through my high desires.

Under the wise advice of my good friend Mathon, the gold lender, I am determined to follow an exact plan that he says will lead any honorable person out of debt and into means and self respect.

This plan includes three purposes which are my hope and desire.

First, the plan provides for my future prosperity. Therefore one-tenth of all I earn shall be set aside as my own to keep. For Mathon speaks wisely when he says:

"Those who keep in their purse both gold and silver they need not spend are good to their family and loyal to the king.

"Those who have but a few coppers in their purse are indifferent to their family and indifferent to the king.

"But those who have nothing in their purse are unkind to their family and disloyal to the king, for their own hearts are bitter.

"Therefore, those who wish to achieve must have coin that they may keep to jingle in the purse, that they have in their hearts love for their family and loyalty to the king."

Second, the plan provides that I shall support and clothe my good wife, who has returned to me with loyalty from the house of her father. For Mathon says that to take good care of a faithful spouse puts self-respect into the heart and adds strength and determination to one's purposes.

Therefore seven-tenths of all I earn shall be used to provide a home, clothes to wear, and food to eat, with a bit extra to spend, that our lives be not lacking in pleasure and enjoyment. But Mathon further enjoins the greatest care that we spend not greater than seven-tenths of what we earn for these worthy purposes. *Herein lies the success of the plan.*

I must live upon this portion and never use more nor buy what I may not pay for out of this portion.

Tablet No. II

Third, the plan provides that out of my earnings my debts shall be paid.

Therefore each time the moon is full, two-tenths of all I have earned shall be divided honorably and fairly among those who have trusted me and to whom I am indebted. Thus in due time will all my indebtedness be surely paid. Therefore do I here engrave the name of everyone to whom I am indebted and the honest amount of my debt.

Fahru, the cloth weaver, 2 silver, 6 copper.
Sinjar, the couch maker, 1 silver.

Ahmar, my friend, 3 silver, 1 copper.

Zankar, my friend, 4 silver, 7 copper,

Askamir, my friend, 1 silver, 3 copper.

Harinsir, the Jewelmaker, 6 silver, 2 copper.

Diarbeker, my father's friend, 4 silver, 1 copper.

Alkahad, the house owner, 14 silver.

Mathon, the gold lender, 9 silver.

Birejik, the farmer, 1 silver, 7 copper.

(From here on, disintegrated. Cannot be deciphered.)

Tablet No. III

To these creditors I owe in total one hundred and nineteen pieces of silver and one hundred and forty-one pieces of copper. Because I owed these sums and saw no way to repay, in my folly I permitted my wife to return to her father, and I left my native city to seek easy wealth elsewhere, only to find disaster and see myself sold into the degradation of slavery.

Now that Mathon shows me how I can repay my debts in small sums of my earnings, I realize the great extent of my folly in running away from the results of my extravagances. Therefore I have visited my creditors and explained to them that I have no resources with which to pay except my ability to earn, and that I intend to apply two-tenths of all I earn upon my indebtedness evenly and honestly. This much can I pay but no more. Therefore if they be patient, in time my obligations will be paid in full.

Ahmar, whom I thought my best friend, reviled me bitterly, and I left him in humiliation. Birejik, the farmer, pleaded that I pay him first as he badly needed help. Alkahad, the house owner, was indeed disagreeable and insisted that he would make me trouble unless I soon settled in full with him.

All the rest willingly accepted my proposal. Therefore I am more determined than ever to carry through, being convinced that it is easier to pay one's just debts than to avoid them. Even though I cannot meet the needs and demands of a few of my creditors, I will deal impartially with all.

Tablet No. IV

Again the moon shines full. I have worked hard with a free mind. My good wife has supported my intentions to pay my creditors. Because of our wise determination, I have earned during the past moon, buying camels of sound wind and good legs, for Nebatur, the sum of nineteen pieces of silver.

This I have divided according to the plan. One-tenth I have set aside to keep as my own, seven-tenths I have divided with my good wife to pay for our living. Two-tenths I have divided among my creditors as evenly as could be done in coppers.

I did not see Ahmar but left my payment with his wife. Birejik was so pleased he would kiss my hand. Old Alkahad alone was grouchy and said I must pay faster, to which I replied that if I were permitted to be well fed and not worried, that alone would enable me to pay faster. All the others thanked me and spoke well of my efforts.

Therefore, at the end of one moon, my indebtedness is reduced by almost four pieces of silver, and I possess almost two pieces of silver besides, upon which no other has claim. My heart is lighter than it has been for a long time.

Again the moon shines full. I have worked hard but with poor success. Few camels have I been able to buy. Only eleven pieces of silver have I earned. Nevertheless my good wife and I have stood by the plan, even though we have bought no new raiment and eaten little but herbs.

Again I paid ourselves one-tenth of the eleven pieces, while we lived upon seven-tenths. I was surprised when Ahmar commended my payment, even though small. So did Birejik. Alkahad flew into a rage, but when told to give back his portion if he did not wish it, he became reconciled. The others, as before, were content. Again the moon shines full, and I am greatly rejoiced. I intercepted a fine herd of camels and bought many sound ones, therefore my earnings were forty-two pieces of silver. This moon my wife and I have bought much needed sandals and raiment. Also we have dined well on meat and fowl.

More than eight pieces of silver we have paid to our creditors. Even Alkahad did not protest.

Great is the plan, for it leads us out of debt and gives us wealth which is ours to keep.

Three times the moon had been full since I last carved upon this clay. Each time I paid to myself one-tenth of all I earned. Each time my good wife and I have lived upon seven-tenths even though at times it was difficult. Each time have I paid to my creditors two-tenths.

In my purse I now have twenty-one pieces of silver that are mine. It makes my head stand straight upon my shoulders and makes me proud to walk among my friends. My wife keeps well our home and is becomingly gowned. We are happy to live together.

The plan is of untold value. Has it not made an honorable man of an ex-slave?

Tablet No. V

Again the moon shines full and I remember that it is long since I carved upon the clay. Twelve moons in truth have come and gone. But this day I will not neglect my record, because upon this day I have paid the last of my debts. This is the day upon which my good wife and my thankful self celebrate with great feasting that our determination has been achieved.

Many things occurred upon my final visit to my creditors that I shall long remember. Ahmar begged my forgiveness for his unkind words and said that I was one of all others he most desired for a friend.

Old Alkahad is not so bad after all, for he said, "You were once a piece of soft clay to be pressed and moulded by any hand that touched you, but now you are a piece of bronze capable of holding an edge. If you need silver or gold at any time come to me."

Nor is he the only one who holds me in high regard. Many others speak deferentially to me. My good wife looks upon me with a light in her eyes that gives me confidence in myself.

Yet it is the plan that has made my success. It has enabled me to pay all my debts and to jingle both gold and silver in my purse. I commend it to all who wish to get ahead, for truly if it will enable an ex-slave to pay his debts and have gold in his purse, will it not aid anyone to find independence? Nor am I, myself, finished with it, for I am convinced that if I follow it further it will make me rich among all others.

The Luckiest Man in Babylon

At the head of his caravan proudly rode Sharru Nada, the merchant prince of Babylon. He liked fine cloth and wore rich and becoming robes. He liked fine animals and sat easily upon his spirited Arabian stallion. To look at him one would hardly have guessed his advanced years. Certainly they would not have suspected that he was inwardly troubled.

The journey from Damascus is long and the hardships of the desert many. These he minded not. The Arab tribes are fierce and eager to loot rich caravans. These he feared not, for his many fleet, mounted guards were a safe protection.

But about the youth at his side, whom he was bringing from Damascus, he was disturbed. This was Hadan Gula, the grandson of his partner of other years, Arad Gula, to whom he felt he owed a debt of gratitude which could never be repaid. He would have liked to do something for this grandson, but the more he considered this, the more difficult it seemed because of the youth himself.

Eyeing the young man's rings and earrings, he thought to himself, "He thinks jewels are for men; still, he has his grandfather's strong face. But his grandfather wore no such gaudy robes. Yet, I sought him to come, hoping I might help him get a start for himself and get away from the wreck his father has made of their inheritance."

Hadan Gula broke in upon his thoughts, "Why do you work so hard, always riding with your caravan upon its long journeys? Do you never take time to enjoy life?"

Sharru Nada smiled. "To enjoy life?" he repeated. "What would you do to enjoy life if you were Sharru Nada?"

"If I had wealth equal to yours, I would live like a prince. Never across the hot desert would I ride. I would spend the shekels as fast as they came to my purse. I would wear the richest of robes and the rarest of jewels. That would be a life to my liking, a life worth living." Both men laughed.

"Your grandfather wore no jewels." Sharru Nada spoke before he thought, then continued jokingly, "Would you leave no time for work?"

"Work was made for slaves," Hadan Gula responded.

Sharra Nada bit his lip but made no reply, riding in silence until the trail led them to the slope. Here he reined his mount and pointed to the green valley far away. "See, there is the valley. Look far down and you can faintly see the walls of Babylon. The tower is the Temple of Bel. If your eyes are sharp, you may even see the smoke from the eternal fire upon its crest."

"So that is Babylon? I have always longed to see the wealthiest city in all the world," Hadan Gula commented. "Babylon, where my grandfather started his fortune. I wish he were still alive. We would not be so sorely pressed."

"Why wish his spirit to linger on earth beyond its allotted time? You and your father can well carry on his good work."

"Alas, of us, neither has his gift. Father and I do not know his secret for attracting the golden shekels."

Sharru Nada did not reply but gave rein to his mount and rode thoughtfully down the trail to the valley. Behind them followed the caravan in a cloud of reddish dust. Sometime later they reached the kings' highway and turned south through the irrigated farms.

Three old men plowing a field caught Sharru Nada's attention. They seemed strangely familiar. How ridiculous! One does not pass a field after forty years and find the same men plowing there. Yet, something within him said they were the same. One, with an uncertain grip, held the plow. The others laboriously plodded beside the oxen, ineffectually beating them with their barrel staves to keep them pulling.

Forty years ago he had envied these men! How gladly he would have exchanged places! But what a difference now. With pride he looked back at his trailing caravan, well-chosen camels and donkeys, loaded high with valuable goods from Damascus. All this was but one of his possessions.

He pointed to the plowers, saying, "Still plowing the same field where they were forty years ago."

"They look it, but why do you think they are the same?"

"I saw them there," Sharru Nada replied. Recollections were racing rapidly through his mind. Why could he not bury the past and live in the present? Then he saw, as in a picture, the smiling face of Arad Gula. The barrier between himself and the cynical youth beside him dissolved.

But how could he help such a superior youth with his spendthrift ideas and bejeweled hands? Work he could offer in plenty to willing workers, but nothing for those who considered themselves too good for work. Yet he owed it to Arad Gula to do something, not a half-hearted attempt. He and Arad Gula had never done things in that way.

A plan came almost in a flash. There were objections. He must consider his own family and his own standing. It would be cruel; it would hurt. Being a man of quick decisions, he waived objections and decided to act.

"Would you be interested in hearing how your worthy grandfather and I joined in the partnership which proved so profitable?" he questioned.

"Why not just tell me how you made the golden shekels? That is all I need to know," the young man parried.

Sharru Nada ignored the reply and continued, "We start with those men plowing. I was no older than you. As the column of men in which I marched approached, good old Megiddo, the farmer, scoffed at the slip-shod way in which they plowed. Megiddo was chained next to me. 'Look at the lazy fellows,' he protested. 'The plow holder makes no effort to plow deep, nor do the beaters keep the oxen in the furrow. How can they expect to raise a good crop with poor plowing?'"

"Did you say Megiddo was chained to you?" Hadan Gula asked in surprise.

"Yes, with bronze collars about our necks and a length of heavy chain between us. Next to him was Zabado, the sheep thief. I had known him in Harroun. At the end was a man we called Pirate because he told us not his name. We judged him as a sailor as he had entwined serpents tattooed upon his chest in sailor fashion. The column was made up thus so the men could walk in fours."

"You were chained as a slave?" Hadan Gula asked incredulously.

"Did not your grandfather tell you I was once a slave?"

"He often spoke of you but never hinted of this."

"He was one you could trust with innermost secrets. You, too, are a man I may trust, am I not right?" Sharru Nada looked him squarely in the eye.

"You may rely upon my silence, but I am amazed. Tell me, how did you come to be a slave?"

Sharru Nada shrugged his shoulders, "Anyone may become a slave. It was a gaming house and barley beer that brought me disaster. I was the victim of my brother's indiscretions. In a brawl he killed his friend. I was bonded to the widow by my father, desperate to keep my brother from being prosecuted under the law. When my father could not raise the silver to free me, she in anger sold me to the slave dealer."

"What a shame and injustice!" Hadan Gula protested. "But tell me, how did you regain freedom?"

"We shall come to that, but not yet. Let us continue my tale. As we passed, the plowers jeered at us. One doffed his ragged hat and bowed low, calling out, "Welcome to Babylon, guests of the king. He waits for you on the city walls where the banquet is spread, mud bricks and onion soup.' With that they laughed uproariously.

"Pirate flew into a rage and cursed them roundly. 'What do those men mean by the king awaiting us on the walls?' I asked him.

"'You march to carry bricks to the city walls until your back breaks. Maybe they will beat you to death before it breaks. They won't beat me. Ill kill 'em.'

"Then Megiddo spoke up, 'It doesn't make sense to me to talk of masters beating willing, hardworking slaves to death. Masters like good slaves and treat them well."

"'Who wants to work hard?' commented Zabado. 'Those plowers are wise fellows. They're not breaking their backs. Just letting on as if they be.'

"'You can't get ahead by shirking,' Megiddo protested. 'If you plow a hectare, that's a good day's work, and any master knows it. But when you plow only a half, that's shirking. I don't shirk. I like to work, and I like to do good work, for work is the best friend I've ever known. It has brought me all the good things I've had, my farm and cows and crops, everything.'

"'Yes, and where are these things now?' scoffed Zabado. 'I figure it pays better to be smart and get by without working. You watch, Zabado, if we're sold to the walls, he'll be carrying the water bag or some easy job when you, who like to work, will be breaking your back carrying bricks.' He laughed his silly laugh.

"Terror gripped me that night. I could not sleep. I crowded close to the guard rope, and when the others slept, I attracted the attention of Godoso, who was doing the first guard watch. He was one of those brigand Arabs, the sort of rogue who, if he robbed you of your purse, would think he must also cut your throat.

"'Tell me, Godoso,' I whispered, 'when we get to Babylon will we be sold to the walls?'

"'Why do you want to know?' he questioned cautiously.

"'Can you not understand?' I pleaded. 'I am young. I want to live. I don't want to be worked or beaten to death on the walls. Is there any chance for me to get a good master?'

"He whispered back, 'I tell you something. You good fellow, give Godoso no trouble. Most times we go first to slave market. Listen now. When buyers come, tell 'em you good worker, like to work hard for good master. Make 'em want to buy. You not make 'em buy, next day you carry brick. Mighty hard work.'

"After he walked away, I lay in the warm sand, looking up at the stars and thinking about work. What Megiddo had said about it being his best friend made me wonder if it would be my best friend. Certainly it would be if it helped me out of this.

"When Megiddo awoke, I whispered my good news to him. It was our one ray of hope as we marched toward Babylon. Late in the afternoon we approached the walls and could see the lines of workers, like black ants, climbing up and down the steep diagonal paths. As we drew closer, we were amazed at the thousands of slaves working; some were digging in the moat, others mixed the dirt into mud bricks. The greatest number were carrying the bricks in large baskets up those steep trails to the masons.[1]

"Overseers cursed the laggards and cracked bullock whips over the backs of those who failed to keep in line. Poor, worn-out fellows were seen to stagger and fall beneath their heavy baskets, unable to rise again. If the lash failed to bring them to their feet, they were pushed to the side of the paths and left writhing in agony. Soon they would be dragged down to join other craven bodies beside the roadway to await unsanctified graves. As I beheld the ghastly sight, I shuddered. So this was what awaited my father's son if he failed at the slave market.

"Godoso had been right. We were taken through the gates of the city to the slave prison and next morning marched to the pens in the market. Here the rest of the slaves huddled in fear, and only the whips of our guard could keep them moving so the buyers could examine them. Megiddo and I eagerly talked to every buyer who was willing to listen.

"The slave dealer brought soldiers from the king's guard, who shackled Pirate and brutally beat him when he protested. As they led him away, I felt sorry for him.

"Megiddo felt that we would soon part. When no buyers were near, he talked to me earnestly to impress upon me how valuable work would be to me in the future: 'Some hate it. They make it their enemy. Better to treat it like a friend and make yourself like

---

1. The famous works of ancient Babylon, its walls, temples, hanging gardens and great canals, were built by slave labor, mainly prisoners of war, which explains the inhuman treatment they received. This force of workmen also included many citizens of Babylon and its provinces who had been sold into slavery because of crimes or financial troubles. It was a common custom for men to put themselves, their wives or their children up as a bond to guarantee payment of loans, legal judgments or other obligations. In case of default, those so bonded were sold into slavery.

it. Don't mind because it is hard. If you think about what a good house you build, then who cares if the beams are heavy and it is far from the well to carry the water for the plaster. Promise me, boy, if you get a master, work for him as hard as you can. If he does not appreciate all you do, never mind. Remember, work well-done does good to those who do it.' He stopped as a burly farmer came to the enclosure and looked at us critically.

"Megiddo asked about his farm and crops, soon convincing him that he would be a valuable worker. After violent bargaining with the slave dealer, the farmer drew a fat purse from beneath his robe, and soon Megiddo had followed his new master out of sight.

"A few other slaves were sold during the morning. At noon Godoso confided to me that the dealer was disgusted and would not stay over another night but would take all who remained at sundown to the king's buyer. I was becoming desperate when a fat, good-natured man walked up to the wall and inquired if there was a baker among us.

"I approached him saying, "Why should a good baker like yourself seek another baker of inferior ways? Would it not be easier to teach a willing man like me your skilled ways? Look at me, I am young, strong, and like to work. Give me a chance, and I will do my best to earn gold and silver for your purse."

"He was impressed by my willingness and began bargaining with the dealer, who had never noticed me since he had bought me but now waxed eloquent on my abilities, good health, and good disposition. I felt like a fat ox being sold to a butcher. At last, much to my joy, the deal was closed. I followed my new master away, thinking I was the luckiest slave in Babylon.

"My new home was much to my liking. Nana-naid, my master, taught me how to grind the barley in the stone bowl that stood in the courtyard, how to build the fire in the oven, and then how to grind very fine the sesame flour for the honey cakes. I had a couch in the shed where his grain was stored. The old slave housekeeper, Swasti, fed me well and was pleased at the way I helped her with the heavy tasks.

"Here was the chance I had longed for to make myself valuable to my master and, I hoped, to find a way to earn my freedom.

"I asked Nana-naid to show me how to knead the bread and to bake. This he did, much pleased at my willingness. Later, when I could do this well, I asked him to show me how to make the honey cakes, and soon I was doing all the baking. My master was glad to be idle, but Swasti shook her head in disapproval, 'No work to do is bad for anyone,' she declared.

"I felt it was time for me to think of a way by which I might start to earn coins to buy my freedom. As the baking was finished at noon, I thought Nana-naid would approve if I found profitable employment for the afternoons and might share my earnings with me. Then the thought came to me, why not bake more of the honey cakes and peddle them to hungry buyers upon the streets of the city?

"I presented my plan to Nana-naid this way: 'If I can use my afternoons after the baking is finished to earn for you coins, would it be only fair for you to share my earnings with me that I might have money of my own to spend for those things which everyone desires and needs?

"'Fair enough, fair enough,' he admitted. When I told him of my plan to peddle our honey cakes, he was well pleased. 'Here is what we will do,' he suggested. 'You sell them at two for a penny; then half of the pennies will be mine to pay for the flour and the honey and the wood to bake them. Of the rest, I shall take half and you shall keep half.'

"I was much pleased by his generous offer that I might keep for myself one-fourth of my sales. That night I worked late to make a tray upon which to display the wares. Nana-naid gave me one of his worn robes that I might look well, and Swasti helped me patch it and wash it clean.

"The next day I baked an extra supply of honey cakes. They looked brown and tempting upon the tray as I went along the street, loudly calling my wares. At first no one seemed interested, and I became discouraged. I kept on, and later in the afternoon as people became hungry, the cakes began to sell, and soon my tray was empty.

"Nana-naid was well pleased with my success and gladly paid me my share. I was delighted to own pennies. Megiddo had been right when he said masters appreciated good work from their slaves. That night I was so excited over my success I could hardly sleep and tried to figure how much I could earn in a year and how many years would be required to buy my freedom.

"As I went forth with my tray of cakes every day, I soon found regular customers. One of these was none other than your grandfather, Arad Gula. He was a rug merchant and sold to many households, going from one end of the city to the other, accompanied by a donkey loaded high with rugs and a slave to tend it. He would buy two cakes for himself and two for his slave, always tarrying to talk with me while they ate them.

"Your grandfather said something to me one day that I shall always remember. 'I like your cakes, boy, but better still I like the fine enterprise with which you offer them. Such spirit can carry you far on the road to success.'

"But how can you understand, Hadan Gula, what such words of encouragement could mean to a slave boy, lonesome in a great city, struggling with all he had in him to find a way out of his humiliation?

"As the months went by I continued to add pennies to my purse. It began to have a comforting weight upon my belt. Work was proving to be my best friend, just as Megiddo had said. I was happy, but Swasti was worried.

"'Thy master, I fear to have him spend so much time at the gaming houses,' she protested.

"I was overjoyed one day to meet my friend Megiddo upon the street. He was leading three donkeys loaded with vegetables to the market. 'I am doing mighty well,' he said. 'My master appreciates my good work, for now I am a foreman. See, he trusts the marketing to me, and also he is sending for my family. Work is helping me to recover from my great trouble. Someday it will help me buy my freedom and once more own a farm of my own.'

"Time went on, and Nana-naid became more and more anxious for me to return from selling. He would be waiting when I returned and would eagerly count and divide our money. He would also urge me to seek further markets and increase my sales.

"Often I went outside the city gates to solicit the overseers of the slaves building the walls. I hated to return to the disagreeable sights but found the overseers liberal buyers. One day I was surprised to see Zabado waiting in line to fill his basket with bricks. He was gaunt and bent, and his back was covered with welts and sores from the whips of the overseers. I was sorry for him and handed him a cake, which he crushed into his mouth like a hungry animal. Seeing the greedy look in his eyes, I ran before he could grab my tray.

"'Why do you work so hard?' Arad Gula said to me one day. Almost the same question you asked of me today, remember? I told him what Megiddo had said about work and how it was proving to be my best friend. I showed him with pride my wallet of pennies and explained how I was saving them to buy my freedom.

"'When you are free, what will you do?' he inquired.

"'Then,' I answered, I intend to become a merchant.'

"At that he confided in me—something I had never suspected.

'You know not that I, also, am a slave. I am in partnership with my master.'"

"Stop," demanded Hadan Gula. 'I will not listen to lies defaming my grandfather. He was no slave." His eyes blazed in anger.

Sharru Nada remained calm. "I honor him for rising above his misfortune and becoming a leading citizen of Damascus. Are you, his grandson, cast of the same mold? Are you strong enough to face facts, or do you prefer to live under false illusions?"

Hadan Gula straightened in his saddle. In a voice suppressed with deep emotion he replied, "My grandfather was beloved by all. Countless were his good deeds. When the famine came, did not his gold buy grain in Egypt, and did not his caravan bring it to Damascus and distribute it to the people so none would starve? Now you say he was but a despised slave in Babylon."

"Had he remained a slave in Babylon, then he might well have been despised, but when, through his own efforts, he became a great man in Damascus, the gods indeed changed his misfortunes and honored him with their respect," Sharru Nada replied.

"After telling me that he was a slave," Sharru Nada continued, 'he explained how anxious he had been to earn his freedom. Now that he had enough money to buy this, he was much disturbed as to what he should do. He was no longer making good sales and feared to leave the support of his master.

"I protested his indecision: 'Cling no longer to your master. Get once again the feeling of being free. Act like a free person and succeed like one! Decide what you desire to accomplish, and then work will aid you to achieve it!' He went on his way, saying he was glad I had shamed him for his cowardice.[2]

2. Slave customs in ancient Babylon, though they may seem inconsistent to us, were strictly regulated by law. For example, a slave could own property of any

"One day I went outside the gates again and was surprised to find a great crowd gathering there. When I asked a man for an explanation he replied, 'Have you not heard? An escaped slave who murdered one of the king's guards has been brought to justice and will this day be flogged to death for his crime. Even the king himself is to be here.'

"So dense was the crowd about the flogging post, I feared to go near lest my tray of honey cakes be upset. Therefore, I climbed up the unfinished wall to see over the heads of the people. I was fortunate in having a view of Nebuchadnezzar himself as he rode by in his golden chariot. Never had I beheld such grandeur, such robes and hangings of gold cloth and velvet.

"I could not see the flogging, although I could hear the shrieks of the poor slave. I wandered how one so noble as our handsome king could endure to see such suffering, yet when I saw he was laughing and joking with his nobles, I knew he was cruel, and I understood why such inhuman tasks were demanded of the slaves building the walls.

"After the slave was dead, his body was hung upon a pole by a rope attached to his leg so all might see. As the crowd began to thin, I went close. On the hairy chest, I saw tattooed two entwined serpents. It was Pirate.

"The next time I met Arad Gula, he was a changed man. Full of enthusiasm, he greeted me: 'Behold, the slave you knew is now free. There was magic in your words. Already my sales and my profits are increasing. My wife is overjoyed. She was a free woman, the niece of my master. She much desires that we move to a strange city where no one shall know I was once a slave. Thus our children shall

---

kind, even other slaves upon which his master had no claim. Slaves intermarried freely with non-slaves. Children of free mothers were free. Most of the city merchants were slaves. Many of these were in partnership with their masters and wealthy in their own right.

be above reproach for their father's misfortune. Work has become my best helper. It has enabled me to recapture my confidence and my skill to sell.'

"I was overjoyed that I had been able, even in a small way, to repay him for the encouragement he had given me.

"One evening Swasti came to me in deep distress: 'Your master is in trouble. I fear for him. Some months ago he lost much at the gaming tables. He pays not the farmer for his grain nor his honey. He pays not the money lender. They are angry and threaten him.' "

"Why should we worry over his folly? We are not his keepers,' I replied thoughtlessly.

"'Foolish youth, you understand not. To the money lender he gave your title to secure a loan. Under the law he can claim you and sell you. I know not what to do. He is a good master. Why? Oh why, should such trouble come upon him?'

"Nor were Swasti's fears groundless. While I was doing the baking next morning, the money lender returned with a man he called Sasi. This man looked me over and said I would do.

"The money lender waited not for my master to return but told Swasti to tell him he had taken me. With only the robe on my back and the purse of pennies hanging safely from my belt, I was hurried away from the unfinished baking.

"I was whirled away from my dearest hopes as the hurricane snatches the tree from the forest and casts it into the surging sea. Again a gaming house and barley beer had caused me disaster.

"Sasi was a blunt, gruff man. As he led me across the city, I told him of the good work I had been doing for Nana-naid and said I hoped to do good work for him. His reply offered no encouragement:

"'I like not this work. My master likes it not. The king has told him to send me to build a section of the Grand Canal. Master tells

Sasi to buy more slaves, work hard, and finish quick. Bah, how can any man finish a big job quick?'

"Picture a desert with not a tree, just low shrubs and a sun burning with such fury the water in our barrels became so hot we could scarcely drink it. Then picture rows of men going down into the deep excavation and lugging heavy baskets of dirt up soft, dusty trails from daylight until dark. Picture food served in open troughs from which we helped ourselves like swine. We had no tents, no straw for beds. That was the situation in which I found myself. I buried my wallet in a marked spot, wondering if I would ever dig it up again.

"At first I worked with good will, but as the months dragged on, I felt my spirit breaking. Then the heat fever took hold of my weary body. I lost my appetite and could scarcely eat the mutton and vegetables. At night I would toss in unhappy wakefulness.

"In my misery, I wondered if Zabado had not the best plan, to shirk and keep his back from being broken in work. Then I recalled my last sight of him and knew his plan was not good.

"I thought of Pirate with his bitterness and wondered if it might be just as well to fight and kill. The memory of his bleeding body reminded me that his plan was also useless.

"Then I remembered my last sight of Megiddo. His hands were deeply calloused from hard work, but his heart was light, and there was happiness on his face. His was the best plan.

"Yet I was just as willing to work as Megiddo; he could not have worked harder than I. Why did not my work bring me happiness and success? Was it work that brought Megiddo happiness, or were happiness and success merely in the laps of the gods? Was I to work the rest of my life without gaining my desires, without happiness and success? All of these questions were jumbled in my mind, and I had no answer. Indeed, I was sorely confused.

"Several days later, when it seemed that I was at the end of my endurance and my questions still unanswered, Sasi sent for me. A messenger had come from my master to take me back to Babylon. I dug up my precious wallet, wrapped myself in the tattered remnants of my robe, and was on my way.

"As we rode, the same thoughts of a hurricane whirling me hither and thither kept racing through my feverish brain. I seemed to be living the weird words of a chant from my native town of Harroun:

> *Besetting a man like a whirlwind,*
> *Driving him like a storm,*
> *Whose course no one can foliate,*
> *Whose destiny no one can foretell.*

"Was I destined to be ever thus punished for I knew not what? What new miseries and disappointments awaited me?

"When we rode to the courtyard of my master's house, imagine my surprise when I saw Arad Gula awaiting me. He helped me down and hugged me like a long-lost brother.

"As we went our way I would have followed him as a slave should follow his master, but he would not permit me. He put his arm about me, saying, 'I hunted everywhere for you. When I had almost given up hope, I met Swasti, who told me of the money lender, who directed me to your noble owner. He drove a hard bargain and made me pay an outrageous price, but you are worth it. Your philosophy and your enterprise have been my inspiration to this new success.'

"'Megiddo's philosophy, not mine,' I interrupted.

"'Megiddo's and yours. Thanks to you both, we are going to Damascus, and I need you for my partner. See,' he exclaimed, 'in one moment you will be a free man!' So saying, he drew from beneath his robe the clay tablet carrying my title. This he raised above his head and hurled it to break in a hundred pieces upon the cobblestones. With glee he stamped upon the fragments until they were but dust.

"Tears of gratitude filled my eyes. I knew I was the luckiest man in Babylon.

"Work, you see by this, in the time of my greatest distress, proved to be my best friend. My willingness to work enabled me to escape from being sold to join the slave gangs upon the walls. It also so impressed your grandfather, who selected me for his partner."

Then Hadan Gula questioned, "Was work my grandfather's secret key to the golden shekels?"

"It was the only key he had when I first knew him," Sharru Nada replied. "Your grandfather enjoyed working. The gods appreciated his efforts and rewarded him liberally."

"I begin to see." Hadan Gula spoke thoughtfully. "Work attracted his many friends who admired his industry and the success it brought. Work brought him the honors he enjoyed so much in Damascus. Work brought him all those things I have approved. And I thought work was fit only for slaves."

"Life is rich with many pleasures to enjoy," Sharru Nada commented. "Each has its place. I am glad that work is not reserved for slaves. Were that the case, I would be deprived of my greatest pleasure. I enjoy many things, but nothing takes the place of work."

Sharru Nada and Hadan Gula rode in the shadows of the towering walls up to the massive, bronze gates of Babylon. At their approach the gate guards jumped to attention and respectfully saluted an honored citizen. With head held high, Sharru Nada led the long caravan through the gates and up the streets of the city.

"I have always hoped to be like my grandfather," Hadan Gula confided to him. "Never before did I realize just what kind of man he was. This you have shown me. Now that I understand, I admire him all the more and feel more determined to be like him. I fear I can never repay you for giving me the true key to his success. From this day forth, I shall use this key. I shall start humbly as he started, which befits my true station far better than jewels and fine robes."

So saying, Hadan Gula pulled the jeweled baubles from his ears and the rings from his fingers. Then, reining his horse, he dropped back and rode with deep respect behind the leader of the caravan.

About the Author

GEORGE SAMUEL CLASON was born in Louisiana, Missouri, on November 7, 1874. He attended the University of Nebraska and served in the United States Army during the Spanish-American War. Beginning a long career in publishing, he founded the Clason Map Company of Denver, Colorado, and published the first road atlas of the United States and Canada. In 1926, he issued the first of a famous series of pamphlets on thrift and financial success, using parables set in ancient Babylon to make each of his points. These were distributed in large quantities by banks and insurance companies and became familiar to millions, the most famous being "The Richest Man in Babylon," the parable from which the present volume takes its title. These "Babylonian parables" have become a modern inspirational classic.